JESUS MAKES THE WORLD TAKES

Finding My Purpose In A World Fighting To Take It

By

Laura I Rodriguez

This book is dedicated First to Jehovah God, his son Jesus Christ, The Holy Spirit, and the Angels. I believe the whole spiritual realm is at work for my good and for that reason I dedicate this book to them.

Secondly, to my grandchildren I love you so much I can't even write this without getting excited! You have made me into the woman I am today! Ever since the day I became a grandmother I became fearless, I started going for my dreams and achieving them!

Because of you I am better, and I strive to be better every day! I pray I always make you proud and that even at my not proudest moments you can love me anyway the way I will always love you!

God bless you always and cover you that you never give up and you always stay in touch with our heavenly father that you always trust him and always acknowledge him, and he will direct your paths.

That if your grandmother gives you something with this book it's the importance of prayer, bible reading, but most important is FAITH! Trust in God!

Lastly, I would like to thank my daughters for always being by my side through it all! Words are not enough for me to express my love for you, I pray that you will always know that I will always be here and that no matter what my love for you is unconditional.

I am so proud of the women you have become, Strong, Intelligent, Independent, Loving, Amazing women! I am honored to be your mother!

IN LOVING MEMORY OF

ALL those who are no longer with us, thank you for all the lessons and all the blessings! My faith and Jesus tell me this is not the end and that gives me so much comfort that one day we will meet again.

Chapter One

My story begins in Trenton, N.J. 1978. My mother was sent to New York when she was fourteen years old after her mother, was brutally murdered by her stepfather in the small town of Utuado, Puerto Rico.

It was a scene out of a movie, my fourteen-year-old mother while holding her baby sister, stood over the bodies of her mother and her stepfather who had killed himself in this tragic murder suicide which would be the beginning of a life that I would be born into, a life that started out with pain as far back as my genealogy goes.

For what I was told by my aunt, my great grandmother, from my father's side, was a slave stolen from Africa. As far back as my story goes even before I came into existence the trauma, the toxicity, the pain, the suffering, it was all here waiting ready for me.All I had to do was be born.

So, I did! September 23, 1978, Mom was watching "The Incredible Hulk" when she went into labor. That became a running joke, since it would match perfectly with my personality.

They say your memory starts at the age of your first trauma. I was four years old when my mother and I went to Puerto Rico for a visit.

While we were there, we would get to see my two older brothers who were separated from my mother when they were very young, before my birth so I was never clear on what were the facts behind the separation. I can only say that I have lived through the pain it has caused the family.

My first memory I have is remembering my chest beating and feeling scared for the first time, my aunt was yelling, and I remember seeing my brother at the bottom of the stairs crying and a mattress on top of him.

It looked as if he had fallen while trying to move it. Whatever the case, I still remember how scared I felt and how worried I was for my brother, and I wonder now why I feel so worried for him?

I felt danger for the first time, little did I know that would be the end of my innocence and the beginning of a journey that would allow me to see God's strength in my weakness even at a young age.

As we arrived back in Jersey from Puerto Rico, I still remember the happiness I felt as my father carried me on his neck at the Newark Airport.

The smiles on all my family's faces as we walked to baggage claim, back then you could wait for your family to arrive at the gate, that would be the last time I would know the meaning of happiness.

Our life was about to be turned upside down. When we arrived home from the airport my sister dropped a bomb on my mother, my father was having an affair with her niece, her sister's daughter.

I still can't imagine the sick, sinking feeling that must have come over my mother as the words came out my sister's mouth. I still hurt for her when I look back.

My mother lost it as any woman would and all I remember was her packing us up and driving us up to Massachusetts to her brother's house to get away as she always did when things got rough, a habit I would quickly pick up.

We stayed there a few days and just like that we were on our way back. When we got home my father was remodeling the house. I remember he was putting in new floors when we arrived, as if that was going to change anything, or would it?

For a very short while it looked as if everything was going to be okay, but that didn't last long at all. My father was not going to change.

History had already shown that this was not the first time he had violated his vows. This would be the second time, and not to name the numerous other women, he was a lady's man.

My father had a way with women and unfortunately, he didn't know boundaries, or he didn't care, either way his actions would affect many others, including me.

I was daddy's little girl, every single night we would go to bed to the Spanish radio station or as my dad called it "La Misora" and I would wrap my little leg around my dad and every night we would do just that.

Unfortunately for me, my father didn't think about our nightly routine or how I would sleep without him. What would that little girl do at bedtime if her Daddy would go? He left.

Mom didn't take it well at all to say the least, first she disappeared. My father came as we searched for her everywhere fearing the worst but praying for the best.

We were all around in the living room. I assume trying to find her when there was a knock at the door, it was a police officer. They had found my mother wandering in the downtown Trenton streets. She was taken to the hospital.

Later, in life my mom told me how she almost drove her car off the bridge from the pain and desperation she felt at that moment. Mom came to her senses and things started looking like maybe we would be okay or so I thought.

As any woman would, my mother was not okay, I remember laying in her bed trying to fall asleep but instead I would just stare at my mother looking out the window crying waiting or better yet wishing for my father to come home.

My mother got wind that my father and my cousin moved into an apartment together, and she found out the location. Most five-year-olds are in bed at night watching cartoons eating snacks, instead my older sister and I were my mother's co-detectives, as we sat in her car parked across the street watching my father's new apartment.

We sat out there for hours, I imagine my mother never thought how that would traumatize a little girl, or how that would affect the rest of our lives.

One night as we left church we were driving home and out of nowhere my mom saw my father's car and of course my cousin was in the car with him. My mother pulled them over. I still wonder why they stopped?

6

Mom popped her trunk, pulled out a baseball bat and attempted to use it on my cousin. Thank God for my Godmother who was in the car and was able to get my mother back into the car and a tragedy was avoided.

Looking back that night could've ended very differently. Shortly after this my father attempted to leave my cousin and come back home but she attempted suicide. She ended up in the hospital. My mother ran to the hospital to check on her niece after all that, which taught me how to love anyway. That was when I understood how love overcomes all things.

My mother gave my father an ultimatum because up to this point, he was going back and forth and playing both sides of the fence, and my father responded by saying "I don't leave women, women leave me."

Those words hit my mom like a ton of bricks as she would later tell me. She realized at that moment that if she didn't walk away and throw in the towel that she would be stuck in this vicious cycle and that if she didn't walk away tragedy would be the only outcome. So, she walked away from the relationship and made her own life.

Sometime later we got on a plane to Texas to "visit" my older sister. My mother, sister, and I got on a flight to Houston where our eldest sister awaited us. We arrived at her house which was stunning to say the least.

For a minute it looked as if everything was going to be okay. I remember playing with my niece and nephew, I was a very young aunt to say the least. I would try to stay in a child's place but unfortunately even at such a young child I knew too much.

I was aware of the reality of adulthood, which no child should ever be exposed to the way I was. Everything was getting ready to change.

I remember my mother standing nervously in my sister's kitchen, she looked like something was weighing heavy on her. I only remember her saying she wanted to talk to me that she had something she needed to say to me.

I must have been six or seven when my mother told me that I had a baby brother. My mother did what she did best; she packed us up and took us to Texas just to run from the fact that her niece had given birth to her husband's son.

She said it was for me, but I believe it was for her. Running was her coping mechanism. I, to the contrary of what everyone expected, was so happy when I found out I was finally a big sister, I couldn't wait to get home to meet him.

When we arrived in New Jersey I was eagerly waiting to meet my baby brother and it was love at first sight. I was born to be a big sister, I was ready to protect him at all costs. The love I felt for him was beyond words till this day he is still in my top favorite people.

I love my baby brother to pieces. So much was happening around this time my father left, and my mother was always a hospitable person. Our house was the go-to house, everyone in the family would be there whether to hang out or to live if they were falling on tough times. That taught me to have a big heart, but it also taught me how dangerous having a good heart is.

One of the people my mother let in was my uncle, her brother. He had a very serious drinking problem and on top of that he also has a disability, he is deaf and mute.

I was seven years old when he started molesting me, and he would continue to do so until the age of nine when my father walked in and caught him in the act. My father slapped him down the stairs and it was a very traumatic event that left me scarred for a very long time.

My father called my mother and she in turn called the rest of her brothers who lived in Trenton, and they did what they did best, they had a family meeting. They interrogated me and my father looked at me and said the most hurtful words I have ever heard, he said "You must have liked it because you never said anything!"

That would be the first time a man would degrade me and make me feel less of a woman although I was a child, I was already a woman, but it would not be the last time, not even close.

The police were never called, nothing was done to him besides he got put out that night. My older sister grabbed me and took me upstairs and put on Disney's Sleeping Beauty. It's weird till this day that it's really one of my favorite movies.

I remember watching it, but praying to God while I watched it, I begged him to help me find peace, no child should ever experience the levels of sickness and anxiety that as a child I was experiencing.

How does a nine-year-old wonder how can my own father think that I enjoyed this when I have been living in fear for the last two years? How can my mother not do anything? Why is she so calm? Doesn't she care? Doesn't anyone care?

I was so confused, and I remember looking at my sister's sad face. She had to be around sixteen and she just says, "I am so sorry, he has been doing the same to me and if I had said something then maybe I could've protected you."

I knew she was heartbroken, but I couldn't help but to think how she could just stand in this meeting and not say anything, nothing, even when my father said his comment, and she was older than me, but little did I know there where hidden secrets in the walls, my uncle wasn't the only abuser in that room and my sister had more secrets than the one she shared on that eerie night. It would be years before I would know the extent of my family's secret and the people behind them.

The next morning, I came downstairs just wishing it was all a bad dream but that quickly became just that. Not only was my mother sitting at the same kitchen table from last night's meeting, but she wasn't alone, her brother, my abuser was sitting with her.

I turned around immediately and ran up the stairs like if someone was chasing me, I ran into the bathroom locked the door and looked around as if a secret door was going to appear and get me out of there, then I looked up and even at such a young age I knew that I only had one person who I could trust and that was God.

I climbed into the empty bathtub. I laid my little body in the fetal position and as I cried, I began to pray. That was the moment of impact. At that moment I knew that there was a secret door that could get me out of any situation at any given time. That if I called on JESUS that he would be that door.

Nine years old and already lived through two major traumas, that's not including the time as an infant I had a very high fever and began having seizures, my parents told me I turned purple and stopped breathing, my father gave me CPR and brought me back to life, it's clear to me the enemy from an early age wanted my life.

 I didn't know then, but the purpose was the calling on my life. Being one of God's chosen I would have to suffer more than most, I would have to carry my own cross, and Lord knows it would be very heavy. I was also living with the question of where was my sister? My whole life I remember everyone talking about my sister who was given up for adoption and at a young age I was trying to figure out a master plan of how I was going to find her one day. I had to find my sister. What did she look like? How was she? Would she love me? Was she being hurt the way I was?

They hated Jesus so of course I would be hated too, more than most for I was chosen. I was being bullied by a few neighborhood girls.

They were all related and there were a lot of them, and it was just me. I had absolutely nobody to protect me inside my house let alone in the streets. My parents were taxi drivers, and they were busy so many days I would walk home from school.

 Back then it was normal to walk home in our neighborhood, for me it was a traumatic event. I would be sick to my stomach. That's how nervous I would get when 2:30 was approaching.

I started to sweat, my heart would pound, and I would get double vision from the distress of knowing I would be bullied once again. I was so scared I would beg my mother to take me out of school, begged her let's run away like we always do when things get hard, she always ran but now I am in trouble, and we can't run. I couldn't understand. I was talking to a wall and she didn't care.

I remember going to my sister and telling her how scared I was one night after I saw her hanging out with the same people who were making my life a living nightmare.

My sister turned to me, and I would never forget her exact words, she said "Tomorrow when you come home from school, and you tell me that you were bullied again, and you didn't defend yourself I'm going to beat you up myself!"

I knew she was so serious but even more I rather get jumped all day before my sister to hit me. She was very heavy handed to say the least, not to discuss all the pain and abuse she was enduring. She is and will forever be my hero. Although I was hurt at the moment, she changed my life because it would be the last time that I would allow anyone, but God to put fear in my heart.

The next day I was walking home from school with butterflies in my stomach, hands and face sweaty, double vision, heart about to pop out my chest and like clockwork my bullies caught up to me as they always did, no matter how fast I tried to get ahead.

The group of girls surrounded me, pulled my hair, called me names the same as always except today I had my sister's voice in my head "I will beat your butt myself if you come home and tell me you got bullied" and something in my head shifted.

My father, my uncle, my mother, my anger, my pain, my desperation, my fear took over and I turned around and began to swing my arms and I did not stop. I took it all out on the main girl.

I arrived at my aunt's house a complete mess shaking, crying, and in need of comfort. It was my first fight, and I was going through so much with my abuse and the separation of my parents.

My aunt did what she did best just that, comfort me, she was and is an angel. My aunt quickly gave me her love on a plate. She is the Queen in the kitchen.

That was her comfort. She would be the reason I have a profound love for the kitchen. I am now the Queen in my kitchen, she is and will forever be one of my favorites.

The bullying didn't stop, it continued and I continued to fight regularly. It would become very normal to me. I realized very quickly that if I did not protect me no one would.

Chapter Two

I continued to fight in the streets to protect myself, and I was good at it. Although I gave them girls a run for their money every time, they wouldn't let up.

 I had to fight one after another. Hood life. It will either kill you or make you stronger. For me it made me stronger. I was different. See I was raised Jehovah's Witness as far as I could remember we were at the local Kingdom Hall three times a week faithfully.

I started reading the bible and many bibles inspired literature at a very early age. I knew I loved God, I feared him, and I knew I didn't want to displease him.

My mother and most of her siblings were witnesses, so the night of the meeting about my abuser, all the siblings that were there were Elders or active members of the Jehovah's Witness organization. It always bothered me how they hid the sexual abuse and handled it internally, or whatever that meant.

I was considered the black sheep of my family and I was the same black sheep at the Kingdom Hall, no matter how much I tried to participate and do everything to fit in I just couldn't. I always felt like a complete outsider.

It could've been because my mother was considered bad association at times, since she was disfellowshipped numerous times. Seems like every time she was disfellowshipped I would get disfellowshipped too.

Imagine being a young child and adults telling their children not to associate themselves with you simply because your mother committed a sin. I remember having determination even at nine, I was determined to please God even if my mother wasn't going to, even if people would make me feel unwanted, I would remember that Jesus also felt those feelings and I would attend meetings by myself.

I would have my mother drop me off and pick me up, they would go out preaching door to door on Saturday mornings, again I would attend by myself and knock-on doors with the congregation even when the adults in my home were not. I felt comfort in God, I didn't want to abandon the only person who was there in the midst of my storms. I was not a normal nine-year-old. I was different.

As I struggled with religion, abuse, my parents' separation, being bullied, and the beginning of what I would later know as depression, things started getting bad between me and my father's new companion.

Although she was my cousin and the mother of my baby brother, we didn't seem to get along at all. I have always been very spiritual and since I had suffered so much at such a little age, I could feel that her feelings for me had changed.

It went from me being a four-year-old sitting on her lap as she played Puerto Rican patty cake with me to now, she despised me, I was in the way.

My father, although he hurt me deeply with his words, always loved me more than anyone. I was the apple of his eye and everyone knew that, so now they were officially starting their family and I was in the way.

Unfortunately, the jealousy did not allow my cousin to welcome me in that family, so a war began. She wasn't the only one who has treated me in a way because of my father, that was like a cancer that spread

13

throughout the family, and sadly I have been the innocent victim of hate, jealousy and envy. They are indeed worse than cancer.

Things began to get extremely uncomfortable, and I was no longer the little scared girl that was willing to allow those around me to hurt me, bully me, or mistreat me. After a few fights I was ready.

Like Tiffany Haddish says "She Readyyyyyy!" At nine I was ready!!

My cousin realized that I adored my baby brother and that I wanted to be with him all the time. That was my happiness, so it began, first she would not allow me to call the house to speak to my dad.

How do you restrain a nine-year-old child from calling her father? He allowed it. He told me just wait until he came to see me, which he did every day, but now that meant I could not see my baby brother. I absolutely had it.

I remember calling over there and asking for my father although I was already told not to call, but that little girl was hurting, angry, and tired of being mistreated. Of course, my cousin answered the phone and the conversation went left very quickly.

It went from why are you calling? To a little angry child cursing a grown woman out disrespectfully with no regrets. I remember she said I am going to tell your brother you don't love him, and it went from bad to worse. At that point she said she was going to come over and tell my mom how I was cursing. All I heard was "Meet me outside!"

A few minutes later she pulled up as she said she would, and nine-year-old me was waiting outside like I said I would be, and the moment her mouth opened to speak all I heard was the words she said over that phone "I am going to tell your brother that you don't love him!"

Those words replayed and I blacked out. I jumped through the window, and I unfortunately put hands on her like I did those girls in the street. Somehow, she started reversing the car, so I quickly jumped out and as she pulled off, I grabbed a brick and threw it at the car, missing thankfully, but still throwing it nonetheless.

Another moment of impact, something clicked in my head at that moment, and I started to change for the worse mentally. I started feeling something I never felt, I started not caring anymore, I had nothing to lose.

I was a whole grown woman stuck inside a little girl's body. At nine years old I could clean a house, do laundry, hang them outside "the good old way," pick them up, iron them, put them away, cook full meals not hot dogs, make my mother's coffee in the morning, and start her car. I would write my mother's checks for all her bills and balance her checking account all by the age of nine.

I was a woman. Everything was changing quickly, and my mind went from the mickey mouse-club to a very dark place. I remember lying in bed crying for hours begging God to intercede because at such a little age I was having suicidal thoughts.

I would lay wondering if I would die, would they care, but during all that it was as if God would just wrap his arms around my little body that would always find itself in a fetal position and would hold me and make everything alright. Even as a child he gave me strength.

It seemed when things were going okay something else would happen. My mom, my sister and I were in my mother's room hanging out watching TV and organizing like always, my mother had a habit of making a mess just for us to clean it and then call it organizing.

Out of nowhere the phone rings, I could tell by my mother's tone that it would be a phone call that would change my life, and it was.

My beautiful Grandmother, my father's mother, the woman who made me feel loved, the woman I was named after had passed away.

My world shattered, I fell to the ground, and I screamed and cried inconsolably. I could not believe the most important woman in my life was gone.

I still remember how she wrapped her arms around me the day I thought my grandfather was dead because he wasn't moving on the patio, he was just lying there and she told me "Come on don't pay attention to that crazy old man!"

No more would she be waiting on the porch when we arrived in Puerto Rico, no longer would she keep me inside watching soaps with her while my cousins were allowed to stay outside, no longer would she rub Vicks on my chest for my cough I would always get, no longer would she rub alcohol on my mosquito bites, and no longer would she hug me and tell me that she knows people treat me unkind. Then she reminded me that she loved me more than anything and that I was very special to never forget it. I was devastated!

My father got us plane tickets and we immediately flew out to Puerto Rico to say our goodbyes to our Queen.

In Puerto Rico, the body was prepared and then returned to the home where the wake would happen, the living room was turned into a funeral home for two to three days until it was time to go to the cemetery for the burial.

You can imagine how difficult it would be for a nine-year-old who was already dealing with mental illness to now sleep in a house where your grandmother is in a casket in the living room.

I cannot say that made my mental illness better at all. Instead I came back from Puerto Rico as my sisters and cousins loved to call me "GROWN."

Things did not get better. The war between my father's new house and our house continued. I was a bit of a tomboy, I loved to play with the boys since the girls seemed to hate me. I would climb trees, ride on the handlebars, anything the boys were doing I was in.

As time went on and I fought so many times, the girls decided to "be friends" with me and at that age you wanted to fit in so bad I was ecstatic!

Same girls that made me miserable were now in my house spending the night, going out for pizza, playing dress up, and doing all the things I only wished for. The one thing I knew nothing about was boys, I did not like boys, I did not have those interests.

Quickly I realized that I was different because while they were looking out the window crushing on the older boys who stood on the corner selling drugs, I was crushing on one of the girls.

At that early age I was devastated I hated myself, I was a disgrace, disgusting, the bible says God hates homosexuality, and although I did not really understand what homosexuality was, I knew that God was not pleased with how I was feeling.

I started drawing away from God, I started pushing away from the Kingdom Hall, I started shutting down, and my depression was getting worse.

Instead of dealing with my feelings, I convinced myself that I had to push those thoughts away that I could not like girls, I had to stop it immediately. It was my guilt that made me so depressed I believed.

It was because I had found a VCR tape in my living room and I innocently played it, turned out to be porn, and I did not remove it, I watched for longer than I should've.

I knew it was wrong, it felt wrong, but I watched anyway. Thoughts ran through my head like why my uncle did these things to me? Why did I have to feel this way, why couldn't I die? I hated living. I could not turn to God because how could God even look at me?

How could he even hear my prayers when in my mind I was garbage. Feelings that I would battle up to today, I thank God that I finally accept who I am, God knows who I am, and how I feel and he loves me anyway.

I became angrier. I was constantly fighting with my cousin and her sisters! A ten or eleven-year-old girl going head-to-head with grown women.

Noone defended me, no one protected me, just a child feeling like the entire world was against me. One day the same girls that were now my friends were now my enemies again, I could not win with them.

I remember them coming to the house and it was a group of them, and I remembered that scared, threatened feeling again, I was terrified. They would never know.

I was cornered, and I thought to myself before I let these girls jump me we'll go to war! The anger began to take over me, and it happened!!! I became "The Incredible Hulk!"

I saw a bunch of glass bottles in the recycling bin, and I began throwing bottles at these girls! As the bottles started crashing, they started running, except for one, always the tough one, so I ran up and punched her on her nose. That was the end of the war between me and the girls across the street.

If I thought it could not get worse, it totally could. I started Junior High and I still had signs of a kind hearted little girl who's only earnest desire since she could remember was to please God.

I remember praying to God that Armageddon would not come and destroy me. The thoughts of Armageddon were destroying me internally, I was suffering from severe anxiety thinking that my thoughts would be the reasons I was going to be destroyed.

I'm not sure if that pushed me away from God, or brought me closer? All I know I still couldn't catch a break.

I remember my mother not having money to buy me any school clothes and I wanted to die! How can I start middle school in the hood where all that matters is what you were wearing. I was a mess.

My mother finally says I will take you to Clover's if you know, you know. Like saying I am taking you to Kmart, to make a long story short. I found a turtleneck and some cowboy boots for my first day of school in "the hood." Trenton, NJ was not forgiving to say the least.

Middle school would be the beginning of a whole new level of problems and this time Ya'll I was NOT READY!!!

These boys were different; they did not look at me like the boys on the block that I was raised with and played with. Immediately something clicked and I realized I was pretty. The girls hated me because the boys thought that I was pretty.

It was not long before my boxing days would return, and they would be at an all-time high. What was left of my innocence was getting ready to disappear. I was getting ready to enter a new door that would come with a new level of anger, violence, disrespect, hate, and addiction. It would also come with many great memories, friends, and love.

I was quickly settling in this new scary thing called middle school. I was making new friends very quickly but just as quickly I was making enemies.

 I was feeling those same feelings that I felt when I was nine years old the butterflies, the sweats, and the heart palpitations. This feeling was one I dreaded.

 I knew immediately that I would have to either stand up for myself and fight or be in a worse situation because this was not elementary school and we were not nine, this was like prison if you do not make a name for yourself, you will be someone's girlfriend.

The choice had to be made. I was fighting regularly; it was not long before I made a name for myself "Crazy!" I took it with pride, you had to be crazy to survive and crazy I was.

 I did not hesitate to punch anyone if I felt threatened in any way, form or fashion. I was in trouble more often than my mother preferred to say the least. The popular kids took me in quickly. I fought my way in of course, next thing we went from fighting to introducing me to cigarettes, alcohol, weed, and boys. Even driving in reverse on a one way! What a blast! I would not even remember the person who walked into middle school, she was gone as fast as she had arrived.

It is true what they say, "Throw me to the wolves and I'll come back leading the pack!" The fact is that I was thrown into the wolves as a child, and I was a walking time bomb.

I even beat a girl up at my first freestyle concert. Five police officers dragged me out of there. My poor cousin was probably thinking she should have known better than to bring my crazy butt.

My mental illness was at an all-time high, the problems at home were not letting up. My mother was in and out of relationships, my father was still gone, no one cared about the abuse, the loss of my grandmother, addictions that were running in my family, and the confusion of my own sexuality.

I was a troubled girl, completely lost and the school system was no help, teachers were not equipped to deal with someone like me. I seemed unapproachable and disrespectful when it was a call for help.

If a teacher would not allow me to use the restroom when I needed to go, I would black out, throw chairs, yell, scream, slam doors, walk out of classrooms, punch lockers. My hands would be swollen from punching lockers all the time and it became normal for me. Black and blue cut up fists were my norm.

I would be home suspended more than not, either from one of my episodes or from fighting which was all the time.

I even had a fight at the kingdom hall parking lot, beat the poor girl up there, and then beat her up the next day at school too. Teachers got hit, it was a mess. I was on a path to self-destruction and I did not even care.

I just knew God hated me and I was going to die because I was the worst sinner in existence, so I told myself. The leaders at the church made their disappointment and disgust with me truly clear.

I could see how tired my parents were with my behavior and I could care less. "Pass me a Newport" was my thoughts. Twelve years old and already addicted to cigarettes. Weed and alcohol were my medicines and at that age I started partying and living my life like I was twenty-one and there was nothing anybody could do to me or about me! It was a problem that no one was going to solve!

Chapter Three

So many thoughts constantly running through my mind, it was like the hamster never stopped running. Depression, suicidal thoughts, anxiety, panic all part of a regular day.

They say you're stuck at the age of your first major trauma, I was still four crying for my daddy to come back. The pain from all the violence, the rejection, the lack of protection I felt, the loneliness it all ran through my head.

I would picture my mother looking out the window crying for my father. The stitches on her lip the time she got in that car accident that traumatized her, because a little boy was hit. The tears in my mother's eyes, the pain in her heart, and the helplessness were always overwhelming.

Seemed that I carried her pain, my pain, my sister's pain, my brother's pain, and the pain of losing my grandmother meanwhile everyone was moving on, but I could not. I was traumatized.

I was fighting so much in school my mother already knew that she would have to come pick me up early. We would make appointments; she was a cab driver.

I would tell her, as I applied the layers of Vaseline on my face, "please be around this area at this time because today I am going to fight."

I remember how my mother would just stare in disbelief and say "Again?"

I would give her a matter of fact look, as I continue to suit up for the next fight. Trenton schools were no joke, you had to fight it was no other way.

You had to get it. Survival and dysfunction were a recipe for disaster. I was a walking time bomb, and my mother could tell.Our relationship started getting very rocky, the anger I was holding in from all I had been through, was starting to come out. My disrespect landed my mother's hands on me.

I remember one day I was trying to make her understand the pain that was running through me, and she has never been able to hear me through her own guilt and pain.I was going off about all the nights I had to sleep at what I like to think as my Godmother's house, I had a twin size bed there that is how much I stayed, I practically lived there.

My Godmother and her daughters couldn't have been more family if they were blood. My Godmother, may she rest in peace, taught me everything I needed to know about God. His love for us, his desire to have an intimate relationship with him, salvation through Jesus Christ, his return, life on earth after his return, and last Revelation 21:4 "And God will wipe away every tear from their eyes; there shall be no more death, nor sorrow, nor crying. There shall be no more pain, for the former things have passed away."

She loved me so much I was her negrita. God was so loving that he gave me a mother when I felt motherless, and he blessed me with sisters when I felt sister less. I will always be grateful for them.

Going back to that night I remember using the phrase "I'm going to tell my father", I will never again. My mother came up the stairs and caught me at the bottom of the attic stairs where I was trying to get away, she physically told me why I should never threaten her again. I remember thinking even my own mother punches on me.

We discipline our children because we want them to respect us and we think we need to, that is what generations have taught us, but my life has shown me that violence of any sort will not resolve any issues.

Looking back on my daughter's point of view I just wanted her to listen, to hear me, to help me, to protect me, to love me, and to comfort me. As a mother all she wanted was my respect, my obedience, my compassion, my understanding that she was going through it too.

She too lost her mother; she was 14 when she was sent to NY to be a housemaid and by the things, she has told me she was also abused. She was dealing with her divorce, and the betrayal of her own flesh and blood who she would do anything for.

The guilt of losing her two sons, the guilt of not being able to protect not one but three daughters to abuse under her own roof by close family members while she was out working trying to make a living.

So how does she deserve blame? She deserved compassion, love, and loyalty. But I could not see past the fact that her loyalty stood with her brother and not me, her loyalty stood with the men that abused my sisters and me. She allowed them to continue to live within our circle. The fact that her brother was not stopped gave him an opportunity and he struck again, abusing other family members.

They continued to allow him around. How can you have compassion when all you feel is anger? Hurt? I felt let down and abandoned.

When she hit me that day, it turned into more anger, I got worse. I was tired of trying so hard to balance God and Humans, to live right by the law and to love those around me when all I felt was hate and pain.

Everyone around me judged me. I had what they called a "worldly spirit" . I loved hip hop, I loved the culture, I dressed in what they considered a "worldly fashion," and I talked "hood." I was too "Black."

I was the "Black sheep of the family" or "The ugly duckling." I did not fit in at all. I never could understand why? Even though I was looked at as an outcast and someone not pleasing to God, I continued to read my bible in my secret place, so I could find out for myself.

In my readings I found that unlike what I was feeling and being told there was a God who was putting all my tears into a bottle and he had them written in his book - Psalms 56:8.

So, between my Godmother and my reading I maintained faith - Hebrews 11:1 "Now faith is the substance of things hoped for, the evidence of things not seen. "

Having faith in such a dark place like where I was heading was extremely hard, it seemed like most of the people who represented God for me were not anything like the God I knew.

My father was now expecting his second child with my cousin, and it was a girl, so the pressure was on for my parents to divorce so they could get married before my sister was born.

It put a lot of stress on my mom even though she was living her life as well. She was seeing someone else and wanted to get remarried. So, they got divorced, they both got married all quickly and my mom's marriage did not even last a year.

Shortly after, she started dating the only man that I will ever give the title of stepfather too. He was amazing, together they made you want to be in love, my stepfather spent time with us, took us out, and showed us what family was supposed to feel like.

It was feeling like everything will be okay. Then my mother decided she wanted to get right with God and that she was going to break up with him or separate so that she could get back into the kingdom hall and that if he loved her then he would become one of Jehovah's Witnesses and marry her.

Well needless to say that kind of pressure would not sit right on most people, and it did not sit right with my stepfather. He was devastated and so was I. He left and never came back. I saw him a few times after that.

My mother was back as one of Jehovah's Witnesses and back to what she did best when things were not going as planned or were getting tough. She ran, except this time it was not just a short trip. This time she sold our house to my dad and my cousin to raise their new family in.

The house I lived in since I was one years old, the house that shared my worst and best memories, the house with my name engraved in the tree up to this day, was about to be handed over to my father and we would be getting on a plane to Texas to live with my eldest sister.

We were leaving our home, the only home I ever knew to go to a new state across the US where I knew no one. The worst part for me was that we were not fully moved out and we still had time before we had to legally be out the house and my cousin started moving things in, and my mother allowed it.

She even brought a small pool, filled it up with water and put my baby sister in it to play, set up a chair and just hung out in our yard to add salt to the wound. I never forget walking in the house, up the stairs to my room feeling completely sick to my stomach, I wondered what had my

24

mother done? I knew it was a mistake that I would look back with regret on. It was.

We arrived in Texas to stay at my sister's house and that worked out for a whole two weeks before our life as gypsy's would continue.

We had a huge falling out with my sister's husband and my sister, they called the elders of the church like they always did for everything, and everything was to stay inside the house.

You did not say anything to anyone. That is how everything was dealt with. My mother was upset with the results, and she took me and my other sister and we walked to a Chinese restaurant within walking distance to my sister's house.

We ordered our food, then we sat on the sidewalk outside the restaurant like homeless people and cried and ate. Those were the worst moments, but the best moments because at that moment we only had the three of us and we had to survive and that is what we did.

My mother quickly went out the very next morning and found us an apartment and moved us right on out of my sister's house. I know that was very painful for them both, for all of us, coming from so far after not being together for so long.

I was four when my sister got married and moved away, so ending up like this so quickly was heartbreaking for all. In life there is a lesson no matter what, for me my mother was my lesson no matter how hurt I was at that moment I could only see the resilience in her.

How she made a way for us and how she was determined to change her life around. My mother wanted to love me, and she wanted to make things work with us. I was willing to try.

At that moment we had nothing, no furniture, nothing. But we were happy. We finally were seeing life through a different eye, we never been this low before. It made me grateful, but it also made me miss my father because no matter what one thing never changed, I was still in my heart Daddy's little girl, and I could not live without my dad.

I started school in Texas. That was a terrifying experience even for me. Like always I would figure it out and I did.

I was starting to get settled into my school when we got the call my fourteen-year-old cousin was shot in her head and murdered by her thirteen-year-old boyfriend. That put a toll on our family.

I had never met my cousin, her mother is my mother's youngest sister, the one my mother was carrying as she stood over her mother's body. Now tragedy struck again.

This really affected me personally, it seems like death, tragedy, pain, and suffering were always lurking around me. After that I started getting really depressed again, I was constantly crying begging my mother to take us back home. I did not want to be away from what I believed was home anymore, but where would we go?

My mother made some calls and next thing we were on a flight to New York to live in Long Island at my uncle's house. Another Jehovah's Witness uncle who was what I can say nicely, strict.

If I thought times were tough in Texas they were just getting started. We stayed with my uncle for a few months, and I can honestly say that although my uncle was strict, he was very fair.

He gave us stability and although I could not appreciate it then, I appreciate it now. I appreciate how he made us peel potatoes a few times a week and made us eat dinner together at the table every night.

We had to read our bible and go to the weekly meetings, because all those things that irritated me then, built character. It would be something I would carry for the rest of my life and something I would later instill in my own children.

Things were moving along, I was getting comfortable in my new school, I was making friends, and even started hanging out with the youths at the kingdom hall. I was starting to fit in for the first time.

Then quickly out of nowhere we were packing and moving to Trenton. Back to my hood, back to the drama, the memories, and all that I thought I had finally gotten away from, but nope here I was again back on Second St.

My mother rented an apartment downstairs from my aunt's house and three blocks from my father's house, our old house. I did not know if I was happy or scared but either way, I was home.

I adjusted very easily to our new home since it was my aunt's apartment, and we were raised in the building our whole life, so it was always lived in by a family member.

I felt very at home there. It is crazy how God puts you at the right place with the right people at the right time. I was still fighting my mental illness and was having a tough time dealing.

My cousin who lived in the attached apartment was an angel sent from heaven to me. He made it his business to talk to me, to encourage me, to show me I am loved, but most importantly to make me laugh.

He was there to teach me that it is okay to be silly, matter fact it is okay to be silly as hell! He taught me that it was okay not to have it all together and that it was even more okay to act like a big kid no matter what age you are and the goofier the better.

I will forever be grateful to him for that. He saved me but unfortunately was not able to save himself. He later passed away due to an overdose, which reminds me that the people who spend the most time healing others, need the most healing. It is extremely hard being the strong one, but he did, and he was amazing at it.

Before we left for Texas there was this boy in our neighborhood and every single time, he would try to get my attention, I would shut him right on down.

I did that repeatedly maybe because he was the neighborhood's lady's man to put it very nicely. To me he was nothing to talk about, but the one thing I can say he was persistent, and consistent.

Before I left for Texas, I talked to him briefly after forever it seemed like, but then I left and we cut ties which I was great with, because I was honestly never interested.

I really hated this guy. When he found out I was back he picked up where we left off. He was not going to give up and he made that clear, so I agreed to give him my phone number and reconnected, a decision I would live to regret.

Chapter Four

So here I am twelve years old and back in Trenton again, the beginning. You always gotta go back to the beginning no matter what. There is no Z without A. The late-night phone calls started; I was talking to this boy until we fell asleep. I was intrigued at the fact that the boy who was known to be on the block all day was coming in the house early to talk on the phone with me.

See when we talked the first time before I moved to Texas, I lived right across the street from the corner store where they hung out all day and there was a payphone on the corner so I would look out the window and he would be waiting by the phone.

Everyone knew the pay phone's, phone number (609) 695-8883 if you know, you know. It was the only free payphone that accepted calls like a house phone and these boys used it just exactly like a house phone, we would be on the phone for hours.

We did not have cell phones back then, all we had was a house phone or as they call it in the south a landline.

My mother hated him so he could not just call so we would set up times to call and talk back then you were sitting by the phone at whatever o'clock. Then we had the clear phones that lit up so we would turn the ringer off so we could sneak late night calls. Whispering all night so my mom would not wake up.

We started getting so close I told him I had been cooking since I was 9 years old and next thing you know twelve-year-old me was cooking dinner for this boy and giving it to him through the kitchen window.

My mother was super strict. I was not allowed anywhere, could not even go outside without her losing it, she was old school.

I tried to understand because of everything we had been through, but I could not understand why protect me so much from the outside world when the damage had already been done and in our own home.

That is why I understand that saying so clearly now "Do as I say, not what I do" well that is a bunch of crap and I say that from a mother's point of view. You cannot just tell your kids to do the right thing and try to embed that in them, if you're not living right. I know from experience.

I was starting to fall victim to the lies and the lines that this boy would tell all the girls. The reason I hated him so much in the beginning is because I saw with my own two eyes how this boy would dog out all the girls, including a close family friend.

I used to tell her to leave that boy alone. He is not worth it, so young, and already thinking so deep. I warned her over and over, but somehow, I became the next victim of this boy. I would be the worst victim of all. I would suffer more than I could ever imagine.

So, I forgot about everything I told the girl, and I was in too deep. I was now his girlfriend officially.

The calls, the food, the sneaking around South Trenton to meet for a quick minute, or some days I would get lucky, and my mom would let me go to my sister's house, Down Bottom the lower part of South Trenton.

My sister lived in the alley called Hills Place and all the boys hung out in the alley drinking, smoking weed, and shooting dice.

So, it was hard to get my mom to let me go there, but some days I would go, and we would take advantage. We would make out on the side of my sister's house, but it would never go any further. I made it clear to him I wanted to be a virgin to the day I got married, nothing mattered more than that to me.

I did not want to fail God; I knew what the bible said. I had a trained conscience, that is what we get when we read God's word. He tells us how much he loves us; he encourages us to lean on him for strength and peace, but he also tells us the things that make him happy and sad. I did not want to make him sad.

But the more I started sneaking around, the less I started listening to my trained conscience and the more I started listening to that lonely little girl who wanted to be loved so badly, and this boy had a way to make me believe he really loved me. All beautiful lies.

Things started getting rocky at home, mom was noticing that I had something going on and she knew exactly with who.

There was no fooling that lady, I see how I became a detective.

The more she tried to get in the way of me being with this boy, the more I wanted to be with him. The sneakier I was becoming. I would do anything to see him and there was no letting up.

I ran away twice, my parents lost it. My dad even had a panic attack that was very scary. I felt bad seeing him cry for me, I have never been okay with hurting others.

They found out I was smoking cigarettes and it was a mess. They came up with this amazing idea "We are going to move to Ewing about 15 minutes away from Trenton, but in Trenton that's like an hour because we don't leave the hood.

Of course, now that I was crazy about this boy and they did not approve they could so easily move me away, but when I was crying and begging because I was being bullied, we could not move. I just could not deal with these people. I was so angry.

There was nothing I could do but pack it up again. It was summertime and that meant another new school. I was not looking forward to that at all, but once again I had to put my big girl panties on and adjust.

My mom called her Jehovah's Witness friend and in a blink of an eye she moved us to a two-bedroom apartment, just like that. The one good thing, there was a pool.

Moving did not stop any communication with me and him. If anything we were communicating more, I was now fifteen.

It had been three years of communicating over the phone and sneaking around and he was putting pressure on me to have sex with him, but I was not trying to hear of it.

Shortly I found out he was seeing another girl and I lost it. I could not even hear of it!

 I was different. He promised me he would never hurt me, and I needed to be loved so bad I could not see straight.

He came to see me to try to convince me that I was crazy, and I was imagining these things. We were up in the canal behind the complex, and we were screaming back and forth, and out of nowhere I had a panic attack, it was so bad I passed out.

That was not the first time that I would be in the emergency room for having a nervous breakdown, except this time I was in a white padded room with nothing in it but me.

 I was in the behavioral health side of the hospital where my mother once was. They had counselors talk to me and allowed my mother to take me home.

My mother was so overwhelmed by everything going on. It was not long before she packed up and ran away, leaving me and my older sister behind. Teaching us a lesson, A lesson about what? Abandonment.

I cried the whole time she was gone, but my sister was always good at cheering me up and making a girl's night out of every situation. I love that about her.

 I loved how she took time to teach me how to cook and to be there many times when no one else was. Until this day I look up to her as a mother and a comforter. She always feels like home. One of my favorites for sure.

My mother left for the weekend and came back with the "I hope yall learned yall lesson attitude." We were always waiting with a clean house to prove we had.

I wasn't learning anything. I was getting angrier; I was moving so far away from God I could not even imagine he could love someone like me. I don't even know why I felt that way, but I did.

Summer passed and it was time to start this new school. I only knew one girl and we were not really friends, but she was the daughter of a

Jehovah's Witness, and we were raised in the Kingdom Hall together. We really did not socialize at all.

She was part of the good kids' group; I was part of the do not socialize group. So, this would be interesting.

We got to the bus stop, it was our first day, so we stood together as she had no friends. I was a little taken back cause the school I came from I had made so many friends and we had our own crew, and this was new for me.

Anyway, I did not have a problem being friends with her since I knew how it felt to be alone. Immediately after getting on the bus, I realized this girl had a target on her back, she was getting bullied before I even got there.

That was not good, I was not going to go back to getting bullied. We get off the bus and begin walking in this overcrowded middle school hallway. This girl had a target on her back and since I was with her, so did I.

It was my first day, I didn't even know where I was going. I had to watch my back from this group of girls who thought they were going to bully somebody, but they had no idea they should have picked someone else.

As we walked through the hallways, they began to push this girl and harass me and that did not sit well with me at all. I knew if I allowed this to fly then I would be dealing with this the rest of my time at that school, and I did not come this far to get beat up.

I let them have their laugh and the moment. I figured it would only be right to wait to get suspended on my first day of school at the end of the first day.

Would not want my mom to think that moving was not a success. I waited until the end of the day, I waited to see the group of girls and I let them walk ahead of me.

Back then we had a keychain trend, you would have a big ring and as many keychains you could manage to get, the longer the better.

Mines was bomb, I had worked hard on them keys. Matter fact I used the same keys when I beat up the girl in the church parking lot years before, so it had grown since then.

I walked behind the girls and went right up to the leader of the group and began tearing her butt up with keys in my hands. Once I had her down, I began to kick her and kick her until she was under the school bus.

Well, not only did I get myself suspended, but the girl was also no longer allowed to hang with me.

Also, the title of the girl who kicked the girl under the bus.

The crazy part was that in the other group there was another girl, it was her first day also. She did not know what was going on, she was just trying to meet friends.

She heard it was my first day too and after that performance she wanted to find out what happened.

We became best friends and from that moment on it was us against the world. To this day she is still my best friend.

She was also traumatized from her childhood. She had been shot by her grandfather who also killed her grandmother, and she had the scars from the shotgun on her stomach. I always wondered how anyone could survive that?

I always thank God because I know he saved her for me. She became my sister from another mother and would hold me down through years of pain. Little did I know.

We found out we were neighbors, and we would hang every day, all day. We were inseparable.

Like real sisters we had our share of arguments, we even fist fought one day at the pool, and boy we gave each other a run for our money.We tore each other up.

That did not matter. We were back up each other's butt like real sisters. Her mom worked all the time, so she was always alone, and I was too so we needed each other. Depression was something we were both very used to, with our traumatic lives.

Feeling depressed and lonely I can see why it was not hard for the boy to take advantage of my vulnerability, to lie and manipulate his way back and even convince me to lose my virginity.

I was fifteen years old when I lost my virginity in my mother's house. It was so bad. The disgust I felt, the feeling of desperation thinking I could be pregnant, how was I going to tell my parents that I was a failure?

It felt like the end of the world to me because I had let down God. That made me run away from God even more, he could never love a sinner like me.

I know now that it was the guilt, I was so nervous about the possibility of getting pregnant I felt like I had to tell my mom. So, I did.

With tears in my eyes, I went to my mother to confide in her and she called my father. I begged and begged for her to keep it between us, but she refused.

It explains why I have the type of relationship I do with my daughters. They can talk to me about anything without fear.

My father came over and we sat down at the table like we always did when it was time for family drama hour. I was sitting across from my dad, a nervous wreck.

I had never been so scared in my life. My mother looks at me and says, "Tell him," My dad quickly responded with "Tell me what?," and I just sank in the chair.

I just began to cry immediately, and my dad just looked at me and with a cracked voice said, "Tell me" So I told him.

My father lost it and called me a few choice words in Spanish. My heart sank, I was nine years old all over again, I was reliving that moment when he told me "You must have liked it, because you never said anything."

I could not figure out how the man that I love the most, my father, would be the one who could hurt my soul with words this way. He was beyond angry, my mother told him to calm down, but he quickly left.

He could not stand to see my face. I felt so low, and I would shut down mentally for a while after that.

I had two boy best friends also and I confided in the two of them my situation and they were so upset, they didn't like this boy either.

They were just as bad as my parents trying to convince me to please leave this boy alone but I just wouldn't listen.

After I told my parents about my mistake, they came up with the bright idea to move again. This time to another small town about twenty minutes the opposite direction from Trenton.

You know what that meant, another new school. I already saw how that went and I was not looking forward to it at all.

I finally settled into my school and had lots of friends after a couple more fights. I did not want to start another school, I did not want to leave my friends, and I did not want to move to this town.

I was getting angrier and angrier. The instability was adding to all the frustrations I was already carrying.

I remember before we moved my mother contacted the elders of the church to talk about me losing my virginity, you can imagine how that went. They added on to the guilt and the disgust that my father had already made me feel.

At that point I was over these judgmental people, I was over them looking down on me making me feel less than I already felt, and I lost it. I remember being very disrespectful and telling them that they needed to stay out of my life, and I meant it.

Things were so bad I could not see past the pain; I could not see light at the end of the tunnel. I was so lost, I was a child with no direction, no hope, no guidance, and nobody to get me out of this hole I fell in.

Soon I will find another way to cope.

I did not feel comfortable going to God at this point, I was convinced that the Jehovah's Witnesses were right. My prayers would not go past the ceiling so there was no point in praying.

Moving day came fast, I was heartbroken, I had to leave my sister, my best friend, the one person I could count on, and now I had to leave her.

I was devastated! I watched as piece by piece, box by box they filled the U-Haul. Just like that we were on our way to Bordentown, where a new adventure would begin. I would continue to make bad decisions. boy was I in for a ride.

Chapter 5

Bordentown should have been called Boringtown, because that is exactly what it was, boring. There was nothing cooking except Pizza downstairs from our apartment in the Pizza Shop.

I was settling in okay because it was a beautiful apartment, very comfy and for the first time in a long time I was feeling homey.

I was trying to act right because I was tired of moving, but I couldn't or wouldn't leave this boy alone. We were still holding on strong, with no signs of letting up.

We maintained our regular phone calls and my mother realized I wasn't going to let up, especially now that I had lost my virginity.

So, she decided that maybe it was time to have a sit down with my father, to allow the boy to come visit me at the house. It didn't go well.

My father would not agree, especially when he already had threatened the boy's life with a wrench.

The boy was terrified of my dad, and he was okay with not talking to my father, especially so soon after "The mistake".

It was time to start my new school and anxiety was starting to kick in right on time like it always did, never missing a beat. I did not have a good feeling about it at all.

My first day at the new school wasn't bad at all, it was a small high school and not too many people so I thought that this could work out for me, "Mike Tyson" , as my mother called me.

Well, those dreams were quickly shattered, just as with all the previous schools there was a boy who befriended me. I was always one of the boys so for me it was not an issue, but his girlfriend quickly thought it was more than what it was.

That of course got me suspended very quickly, I was not going to let anyone disrespect me. So of course, we fought.

I had two fights at the new school and although I won, I lost emotionally, I could not do it anymore and now I was sixteen. After the last fight I walked back into Bordentown High and signed myself out as a dropout.

Although I was extremely smart, I could not focus on my schoolwork because I was always fighting. I was disappointed in myself, sixteen and a high school dropout so I went out and got me two jobs and quickly I understood what Independence felt like, I was making my own money.

My father gave in and started allowing the boy to visit me, yes, he was still around. The visits were good but then we started fooling around in my mother's house and I was not going to allow him to milk this cow for free.

I began putting pressure on him, he took my virginity and now he would have to make me his wife. I was determined to get right somehow, someway.

Not long my parents agreed, and they planned our first wedding which I cancelled. They then planned our second wedding and at sixteen years old I was married to this now twenty-two-year-old man. Yes, he was a man.

I look back and wonder how my parents agreed to my ridiculous idea of getting married, but they did, and they signed so I could get married. It was a big event. My parents went all out for my wedding.

We drove all through South Trenton in our limousine hanging out the sunroof and the hood went crazy! They all cheered as we celebrated our big day.

Sixteen married and now we were at my mother's house picking up my bag so we could go to a hotel for our honeymoon, and it was at that moment when we got in the car to go, that the scared little girl appeared.

I did not want to leave anymore; I wanted to go back home and climb in bed with my mom and never leave her side again.

It did not play out that way, we were going to move to his house and things would only get more complicated. His parents had moved to Louisiana so his brothers and him took over the family house and now I would be living there too.

I quickly took up my wifely duties and me and his brother's girlfriend began to cook, clean, and take care of everyone in the house, which grew quickly when three of his brothers that were in prison were released.

It was a full house to say the least. His brothers quickly took me in as their little sister, I was the youngest in the house. His brothers loved my cooking, I was a good cook thanks to my mother, so I was welcomed with open arms.

Two of his brothers were in gangs, so quickly the house turned from a family environment to the meeting house.

They were having their meetings in the yard, we had members over all the time, and I fit right in due to my roughness I had acquired over the years of trauma. Quickly his brother who was also the leader of the gang, offered me the highest rank as a woman,

He wanted me to be their Queen. I quickly refused, I explained to him that I was not the type of girl who could be told what to do or when to do it. Never been a follower, always a leader. That thankfully did not change anything between us, just made him want me to join more. Especially this day.

I was out with my new husband riding bikes. He was riding, I was on the handlebars. We rode by these two men, and they started saying things about how pretty I was.

That did not sit right with my husband, so he decided he was going to be a tough guy and say something. They pulled out a bat and me being who I was, that bat did not scare me!

I went right over there and started going off in their faces! Until I saw a look of confusion on the guy's face. He said, "was that your man? because he left you."

I looked back and he was running down the street, I was so embarrassed. Me being who I was I told them "You guys' better leave quickly he went to get a gun, a big gun!"

All lies but I cleaned it up nicely because they left. I was walking towards the house pissed off, when he came out running with his brothers.

His brothers were ready and quickly asked sis what happened? I responded "your brother left me in front of a bat, that is what happened!"

When I tell you they made a mockery of him that night. Poor guy was the joke of the day. I never got over the fact he left me in front of the bat.

That night I was pissed, his brother came in and sat with me, asked me what was wrong and I explained how I felt. We quickly came up with a plan to get back at him, so I went to his stash and stole his weed and me and his big brother smoked it all in his cousin's jeep.

We were stuck in the jeep for hours, looking like we were cruising but we were just high. It was a story we would laugh at for years, we still talk about it. He was not happy about the stolen weed, and we did not hear the end of it. We laughed so hard it was awesome. I felt avenged.

Soon things started getting crazy at the house two of his brothers began arguing one day and I wasn't concerned because siblings fight, until it quickly escalated! One brother was chasing the other brother with a machete.

That was so scary. The ironic thing was we lived directly across the street from the Trenton State Prison, and these two goofies were running around trying to kill each other right in front of it.

Of course, police were called and before they pulled up, I was in a car with one of the brothers trying to get him out of there because he was on the run for attempted murder. It was a scene from a movie, us hiding the car in a garage and trying to find somewhere to hide. He was crazy, but he was my favorite, and I was going to ride or die.

Things got so crazy after that night, and we could not stay in the house because it was too hot. Police and gang activity had too much going on. We quickly found an apartment down the street and moved into what would be our first home.

We had to bomb it out on day one because the roaches were climbing up the walls, I was so scared, I never dealt with anything like that. We adjusted and with so much going on I didn't even notice I missed my period.

I was cooking dinner one day and I got so sick while cooking, I was vomiting, and it still did not click in my mind that I may be pregnant.

His brother was staying with us hiding from the police, so he was always in the house, unlike my husband who loved the streets.

My brother-in-law quickly pointed out that I should get a test, so I did. My mother took my sister and I shopping for our other sister's wedding. When I told my mom to buy me a test, she was ecstatic.

We ran home and sure enough it was positive we lost it. It was an amazing day. I was sixteen, married and now I was pregnant. I finally would have someone to genuinely love me.

I was sick the beginning months of my pregnancy and thankfully my brother-in-law was there to help me. I felt very alone, he made it fun. We would watch old karate flicks all day, anything to get me through the funk.

My husband would be next door in my sister's yard playing cards and dominoes with all the guys. It was beyond frustrating, but that's hood life and you get used to it fast.

My mother got the opportunity to move to Georgia to work as a living babysitter and that was devastating for me, I had never been away from her for long, how was I supposed to survive without my mother?

Shortly after my sister also moved to Long Island, which was three hours away, this abandonment feeling would not even go away after I was married and on my own.

Police found my brother-in-law, so my only support system was gone and sentenced to six years in prison. I was really losing it; we lost our apartment because my husband did not have a job and I could not work anymore because of the morning sickness that lasted a whole five months. I was beyond stressed.

We moved back into his parents' house and things were a lot better. I was enjoying living with my two sisters-in law. They were a blast.

We cooked together, cleaned together, were pregnant together, had problems with the brothers together, and finally went clubbing pregnant together!

I had a big belly five months, in the middle of the dance floor dropping it low, the DJ said it was a pregnant woman, and wassss!

It started getting harder to act like everything was okay when deep inside I had never been happy with this man.

All he cared about was the streets. He never had time for me or his soon to be child, I couldn't take it so my mom sent for me before I was too far along to fly.

I went to Georgia with my mom for a few weeks and I was at peace. For the first time I saw how life could be, watching the family my mother worked for gave me ambition and goals, desires and wants.

I wanted to be better for my baby, I wanted my child to have a good life, so I got back on the plane and flew back home to fix my marriage.

You would think my husband would be at the airport waiting for me but he wasn't. I figured he would be home waiting for my arrival but he was not. He was running the streets.

My pregnant self, and my best friend, and her boyfriend just walked all through south Trenton trying to find him and when I did an argument escalated and he left me standing there in the middle of the block.

He disrespected me by singing a rap song "Bitches ain't shit but hoes and tricks", this is what I came home to I thought as I stood there thinking where do I go? What should I do? I just got on the local bus and rode to my friend's house, what a life I had made for myself.

This was the song he felt was appropriate for his pregnant wife.

A few days later he would convince me to come back home, and I did. We found a nice apartment over the bridge, the same bridge on the cover of this book.

It is known as the Trenton Makes, The World Takes bridge.

My father helped me furnish it and get everything ready for the arrival of my daughter. The apartment was so cozy everything was perfect, finally we would be the family I was always wanting and desiring.

It was January 1996 when we were hit with a monster blizzard nicknamed winter storm Jonas by the weather channel and known by some as "Snowzilla" because of the damage it caused.

It knocked out power to more than 100,000 homes and businesses and claimed the lives of at least eight people in New Jersey, it was bad. I remember in the middle of the snowstorm I made my husband go out and buy me some sara lee pound cake, I lived off it.

He deserved it, especially with what was coming.

Things were looking up, I was even allowing a Jehovah's Witness to come study the bible with me, I needed God back in my life. I was so scared I was seventeen and about to have my first child, I needed God.

My mother flew in to help me take care of the baby once she arrived, so I was the happiest I had ever been, I was on top of the world. I could not wait to meet my daughter; I just knew I would never leave her or abandon her and no matter what I would always be by her side.

 I could not wait. My mother surprised me with a baby shower, and then my father and my cousin gave me a baby shower it was amazing, our family was starting to be a family. I was grateful.

Nine months and the day came March 11, 1996, I woke up having cramps and they were not going away so I went in for a checkup and they told me I was four centimeters dilated and I was in labor.

We were in active labor around 3:30PM and my beautiful daughter was born at 6:36pm. The room was full. We had six people in the delivery room, it was even recorded.

 I remember the first words I said when she came out was "she's so beautiful!!!"

 I do not think I even saw her right and I knew she was. It was love at first sight to me, all I wanted was my daughter! My husband on the other hand ran out the door by 7:36pm!

Our daughter was one hour old, and this man tells me "I'm going to go celebrate".

I was shocked! This was what it had come down to, me holding my baby girl crying like I did for most of nine months. My poor daughter was affected by my crying more than I imagined.

Two weeks later my mother and I were driving with my daughter in the car. I had my mother driving for me, helping me look for my husband who had left me and his newborn daughter to go hang out.

I was so suspicious, because not even our daughter could stop this behavior, never underestimate your intuition. I found him with another girl at the store, I whooped her ass and about killed him. I was heartbroken, how could this happen to me. Have I not suffered enough?

I took him back immediately, and we moved back to Trenton this time to East Trenton. I was in love with my daughter, I had a camcorder, and I would record her every minute of the hour, I was obsessed.

I could not even worry about him anymore, I needed to focus on my baby. Just like a fresh baptized Christian after time the excitement wears off and you start slacking, and that is what I did.

I loved my baby and I had to take care of her, so I started working to provide for her needs especially since her father went to jail and all we had was me.

My mother would watch her while I worked third shift and while I slept in the morning. That gave my mother time to bond with my daughter and she was in love with her granddaughter.

They were beautiful to watch, and I was so grateful that my daughter was getting her better version, which was completely different then the version I got.

I was spending time together at my sister in law's house because she was still pregnant and my husband's brother was just as bad as he was, so I wanted to support her. Something I would do for the rest of her son's life.

She gave birth to a son who I have helped raise, until this day he is and will forever be my son, and I, his mom. Little did I imagine I would find support myself. Her baby brother became interested in me and quickly I found myself for the first time interested in someone other than my husband and I did not know what to do.

I was falling quickly in lust. No questions asked. I was now an adulterer and giving my husband a taste of his own medicine. The pain he made me feel when my daughter was born, he was going to feel.

I became a very bitter woman, and I was out for revenge. Unfortunately for me the guy was great to me for a short while and one disagreement he had a new girl and now he was on my hit list both these dudes were going to feel me.

So easily I was distracted, I was forgetting my focus, my daughter. Now I just wanted to be in the streets too. I was outside hanging with my baby in her stroller all over south and east Trenton. Started at third street park and ended up at Columbus Park out east Trenton.

I forgot how amazing things were at home with my mom and my baby. I did not want to be good. I was hurt; I was angry, and I wanted to live too.

My husband and I made up. He did not want to see me with anyone else, although I had shared him since I was twelve. We pretended to be happy once again but quickly he was back on the streets, that jail time did nothing to help. I was quickly wondering was this the right decision, trying to fix my marriage?

That quickly came with a price. I was outside the bar screaming and yelling begging my husband to come home with me and my daughter. It was dark outside, and I had to walk back to East Trenton with my baby.

He refused to go, so I left, and I took the walk alone with my baby for about 20 minutes. When I got out of East Trenton I bumped into his cousin and she asked me if I wanted to go to the park and smoke, so I quickly said yes! Big mistake.

We smoked, everything seemed okay until it was time to leave. I realized I did not know where to go, which way I had to go to get home, I had been laced.

I was scared and pushing my baby. I walked up to some random strangers crying telling them I had been laced and I was scared, and I needed to get home.

This big strange man walked me home. I wish I could thank him today.

There was a group of people outside my house, my mom, my sister, my husband, and his friends. I had been gone so long everyone was looking for me.

Just to tell you, when I showed up laced, we jumped my husband out on Hudson St. He should've never let me and his six-month old child walk alone.

I was breastfeeding so they quickly threw me in the shower because I was tweaking bad, called poison control to see about breast feeding. That night, I only made my daughter suffer with my decisions.

I could not breast feed her and it was her first-time drinking milk, all because of a selfish decision that I made just to try to get the attention of a man. Unfortunately, that would not be the first time I would do that, matter fact I would spend many years doing just that.

46

Finally, something good happened! My dad showed up at my house with some exciting news! My sister, who was given up for adoption when she was a baby, had found us and he was going to take me to meet her for the first time!

I could not be happier. I dreamed about this moment my whole life, even when I played barbies, I would play out how our reunion would be, and finally it was here.

I imagined her very classy, and that she would look at me like I was ghetto, but boy was I wrong. I still remember how excited I was seeing her walk out the door with a Jersey, baggy jeans, and some Jordans.

It was immediately clear that she was a lesbian, and to me that was such a relief, I was not the only one who was different. We immediately bonded, a bond that can never be broken.

Things were hard for me financially like always. I was the main provider of my house at such an early age, I was working at the jewelry store, and third shift at a grocery store trying to provide for my mom and daughter.

My mother was so fed up with all the drama and the fighting that although it broke her heart she picked up and moved to Texas with my sister. I felt so abandoned, when I needed her most. I needed her to just get me together, because I was a mess, I was out of control, and she left.

I found my daughter and I a small apartment that I could afford on my own, but I quickly became so depressed with my mother leaving, and no one I could trust with my daughter, so I stopped working.

My husband was in and out of our lives more out than in, his brothers were around more than him to be honest.

His older brother was having a hard time, so I let him stay and he was a blessing to me and my daughter.

It was the best times when I look back, the image of her uncle carrying her to the store to get breakfast is one I keep close to my heart, because it wouldn't always be that way.

His brothers were my family when I felt I had no family, and they truly had my back, I can say that honestly. They all know who they are, and they will always hold a special place in my heart.

The drama had pushed my mother away and losing her was too much for me to handle. I was only seventeen with a young six-month-old baby at a time when I needed her the most.

My life was spiraling out of control, I had no job, no money, and I was losing it quickly. I started hanging out more on the block with my daughter to get away from thinking about my husband, the abandonment, the betrayal, and the pain.

I became promiscuous, something I had never done before. I was looking for comfort, for the feeling of love, and I made a few too many mistakes and got absolutely nothing out of it. Except for the feeling of disgust and the feeling of complete and utter loneliness. I was ashamed and I was hurting, I was tired, and I just wanted my mother.

It was late at night, and I was walking to South Broad St from Down Bottom with my baby in the stroller and I came up the alley way through the cut and landed on Centre St. My husband pops up out of nowhere with the normal disrespect.

He did not want his wife, the cook, the maid, the mother, the women but he did not want anyone else to have her either.

One thing about our hood, news travels fast so he heard or thought he heard and wanted to now degrade me in front of everyone.

This night I was not beat at all, I gave him a few choice words and kept it moving. I was not going to keep chasing nobody.

I paid my own bills and even though things were hard for me, it was only because he abandoned his home for the same streets he is still standing on today.

His decision did not only affect him, but they also affected us, and our daughter. I sadly could not see God at the time I was too blinded by all the toxicity I was surrounded by.

I kept walking in the dark with my baby when this guy that I had never met, which was surprising to me, since I was born and raised in south Trenton, we all knew each other.

He started trying to talk to me and I was fuming because I was just arguing with the husband, so I sent him packing not nicely either.

A few days later I was back on Centre Street with my girls, one who damn near lived with me to keep me company, when the guy from the other night came up smiling being friendly again.

I was thinking "didn't he get enough?" But he did not.

I had calmed down, but I was not friendly. I was tired of being hurt. So, I was not giving anyone the time of day.

My girls and I kept talking and I invited them to come by to my apartment and hang out that weekend and they all said yes, and little did I know they were not the only ones who heard my address.

By the weekend, my whole situation had changed. I didn't have a pot to piss in. I quickly understood poverty and being a single parent. I didn't have enough money to buy my daughter a gallon of milk, I was desperate.

I asked my brother-in-law to watch my daughter while I walked up the street to my cousin's house to ask for milk. When I got there, she had none either, I even forgot about the girl's night I had planned.

My best friend and I walked quickly back home to see where we could get money for milk from. We were approaching my house when that guy I sent packing not once but twice popped up like toast.

He walked up to me and said, "I know you didn't invite me, but I wanted to come to your party." I was so upset I lost it.

I said a few choice words about the party and began to cry. He asked me what was wrong, I was so desperate, filled with shame I told him I needed milk for my daughter, and he went in his pocket gave my best friend money and said, "go to the store and get the milk please" he turned to me and said, "can you give me five minutes of your time?"

I was so ashamed, after how I treated him, he saved me that night. Of course, I gave him five minutes which turned into all night.

He spent the night with me along with a few friends and we had a blast. We ended up making out in the bathroom and it felt different, it felt sincere. The next day he had to turn himself in, he said. So, I figured I would not see him again.

That evening I was sitting down wondering how long he would have to do, when I heard my name.

I looked out the window and it was him looking up with a big smile on his face and said, "they let me go can I come up?" I didn't hesitate.

For the next few months, we stayed lowkey and stayed in my apartment. My brother-in-law had moved out, so it was just us, our best friends and my daughter.

We felt like a little family, four troubled teens trying to figure this thing called life out. We were having a blast. One day I was sitting on the toilet, and he would love to come in and talk for some odd reason.

He was washing his face when he just began pouring water on me with his hands and laughing so hard as I screamed "I'm going to kill you!!!" it would be a moment I would always keep dear to my heart.

My husband caught wind that I was involved with this guy and unbeknown to me they knew each other.

It caused problems for us. This day he was walking out of my house when my husband's cousin came out of nowhere and sucker punched him, he then jumped into his car, and left.

I was so upset, especially since everyone knew except me at the time that he did not play, and it was a sign of complete disrespect.

Especially when he didn't come and destroy any happy home, although we were not divorced, my husband had abandoned the home long before this guy came and stole my heart.

Chapter 6

I knew things were dangerous in the streets for him and me, especially now that someone came to my house to disrespect us.

I wanted to see for myself what my husband's deal was. He was living his best life. Why couldn't I live mine?

Especially when the same man he disrespected was the same man that bought his daughter milk when he was nowhere to be found which was the norm for him.

I had no idea that he had something waiting for me too. I got down to the block, everybody was outside. It was summertime in Trenton, which means we were out there looking like a car show.

I had the mini skirt with the stilettos on cause back then when we came out, we came out, out! Pushing my stroller!

I just wanted to see what was going on, when one of my husband's best friends walks up to me with two big females and immediately begins talking filthy to me.

Next, he spits in my face in front of everyone. I was disgusted that this disrespectful boy could ever.

So, me being me, I put my hand on my face and grabbed all his spit and mushed it in his face. As quickly as I could, I pushed the stroller to one of my "FRIENDS" because I saw his fist coming.

He punched me repeatedly, all face shots as everyone watched and no one did anything. Nothing at all.

I let him finish and then as I stood there looking like "Wonder Woman" in my short skirt and stiletto boots it felt amazing that he could not knock me out or even drop me.

I looked at him as I grabbed my stroller and I said "that's it? That's all you can do? All these dudes out here scared of you and you couldn't even knock me out and I am 120lbs soak and wet? But it's okay cause I'll be back, believe me I'll be back!!"

 I was so angry as I walked away with my baby feeling like wonder woman! That quickly changed as soon as I was far enough. I was that little girl again, being degraded, shamed, and now spit on?

As I cried walking home it hit me like a ton of bricks, only God kept me standing, only God kept me unmovable, this man was punching me like a man and I did not even move with stilettos on!

Then it hit me they spit on Jesus, who am I to feel any way? But who was I fooling? I was destroyed, my own father never put his hands on me like that, how can I let him get away with doing it. So, I called my Daddy, a registered gun owner.

The swollen, black, and blue face was not going to fly with my dad. That man asked me for a description and location and walked out.

I later heard through a witness, my "friend" who also watched and did nothing that my father came back and pointed his 45 in the face of a few guys including the guy who hit me but no one would admit it was him.

My friend told him he was not there to save my father that prison sentence, but I know if they would have pointed him out my father would have pulled that trigger.

It was the first time I saw my father stand up for me. Quickly after that incident, rumors started circulating saying they were looking for me to cut my face, so I would not be pretty anymore.

The hit called for a signature cut from ear to lip. My father got ear of it and was parked in front of my house with his 45, ready!

I had no idea until my friend came running in saying "Girl your dad is outside parked with that thing on the seat ready!" Something had to give. I could not allow my father to go to prison for me.

A few days later my father's wife came to see me terribly upset and said that my father was either going to end up in prison or have a heart attack and that I should think of my younger siblings because they needed my dad.

She offered me a plane ticket for my daughter and I to leave for Texas with my mother leaving in a few days. I could not believe it, I finally found someone who in a brief time made me feel more love than my husband ever did and I had to go. So, I left.

I arrived at my sister's house and immediately my mother had my suitcase wide open and was washing every piece of clothes I bought, because I smelled like cigarettes.

I was so exhausted with life I did not care if she put the whole suitcase in the machine, I went right around the corner, smoked a cigarette and went into my mother's room.

It was an addition outside in the garage with no windows. the perfect dark place to go and shut down for a while, and that is exactly what I did.

My niece became a major support for me. She helped me get out of the funk and back up and live.

My sister and her husband were still Jehovah's witnesses and although I love them dearly, the rules and pressure were too much for a girl who had been through so much already.

I knew no matter what I had to get out. The guy was still calling me, he was waiting on me to get my place and he was going to leave everything behind to make a life with my daughter and I.

I was motivated. I began working as a server doing double shifts and every day after work, I came home with all my tips and I would give them to my mom to save for my place. Things were looking up finally. I was about to start my life. I could not be more excited.

I thought too fast. My husband found out I left and now he wanted to see his daughter. He magically moved to Louisiana with his parents and now he wanted to be a father.

My sister and mother pushed me to go take her to see him, it was a few hours away and they would come. So, I agreed. They knew how upset I was because of all I had been through but they kept saying you're still married and he is your daughter's father.

We got to Louisiana and his family welcomed our family as always with open arms. His mother cooked an amazing meal as she always did. Everyone was happy to see my daughter and it was all I ever wanted for her, a family something I was robbed from.

I was becoming double minded. That quickly I, although in love and wanting more than anything to be with this amazing guy, was being manipulated by a fantasy and a man selling me more lies.

Love won, I was not going to leave my love for a man who got me spit on and hit. We returned home and I was determined to be happy. I was going to keep working, get my place, and he would come, I would get my divorce and we would get married.

That was wishful thinking, while we were in Louisiana he called and my brother-in-law decided to tell him I was in Louisiana with my husband and he used those exact words.

Just like that he put question and distrust in the mind of the person I wanted to share my life with. Unfortunately, he believed him.

He thought I had alternative motives and that was not the case. He never called back and soon he was arrested and did some time. In that time my husband worked his way back with the help of my family and the stories of the perfect little family I told myself.

My daughter was turning two years old and I was two weeks away from giving birth to our second daughter. It was unbelievable I was daily arguing about my child's paternity. The time lapse from me being with the guy to us getting back together was massive. No chances.

Zero possibilities. Still in a period of what should be happiness, I was still trying to prove my worth to the person who had caused me the most harm.

His family came down for the birth of our daughter and it was great until all hell broke loose, we were arguing, his mom, brothers, everyone was yelling. I went right into labor a week early. March 25, 1998 at 230pm I gave birth to my second daughter.

I had been praying again. I prayed for two specific things "Blue Eyes" and "for her to look just like him" so they can eat their words and doubts! God responded he gave me both.

She has beautiful big blue eyes and looks just like her father. Down to her mannerisms. Be careful what you pray for. I fell in love with my baby and I felt so much guilt for what I had already put my first daughter through. I was determined to make things right with my marriage but more importantly with God.

I started studying the bible with the Jehovah's Witnesses and started really drawing close to God but with pressure. I was always trying to meet expectations that God himself has never required of me which put a gap in our relationship.

I just did not understand him yet. I thought I knew God but I had no idea. I wanted to be a good wife, a good mother, and most importantly a good servant of God. It was not enough.

My husband quickly made friends in our apartment complex and it was not long before he went missing in action. Except this time, he would not be holding up the block, he graduated to video games.

He was out all day and night. I continued to push forward, I worked all nine months and now I would continue to provide for my daughters and I.

I would give them the opportunity they deserved. Two years had passed and he had landed a job in our apartment complex as the maintenance guy. A mutual friend got him the opportunity.

Instead of working, he would be getting high, playing video games in other apartments.

My mother had moved back to Georgia to work for the same family. I was alone and exhausted, but still holding on strong. I was two months pregnant and didn't even know it.

I was twenty-one years old when I was baptized as a Jehovah's Witness. I was four months pregnant when I received my GED. I was on the right track, I was focused.

It was not long until our friend could not cover for him any longer and with tears in his eyes he told me "I know how hard this is going to be on you but we have to let him go."

What was I gonna do now? What I did best call my mother. We packed a trailer full of all we could fit in it. I had to give away my two dogs and we headed to Georgia.

We arrived at our own apartment. My mother took care of everything. I was so blessed to have her. I could breathe thanks to her.

I quickly got a job at the daycare my mother was working part time in. I was pregnant with what I called my "miracle baby," but still changing diapers all day.

I can honestly say it wasn't anything like I pictured myself to be at twenty-one. I was now convinced that my husband was going to get himself right.

This was now the third new state and the third fresh start, I was sure this was the time he was going to change. I bet you're laughing; you should be because I was dumber than rocks.

He made new friends faster than I could deliver our baby. More video games and more lonely nights for me and my daughters. Thankfully, I had my mother's support.

December 1st, 1999, I gave birth to my third daughter, my miracle baby and the one he said I stole. He did not want any more kids but I did. Sadly, he made it known to us for years to come.

A rejection my daughter would carry throughout her life. After hearing him say it repeatedly.

Sadly, I found out that my husband wasn't only entertained by video games but he was also entertaining other women.

I could not see past the pain. I was not able to think about how far I had come, how much I had accomplished for my daughters and how much I had to lose.

I began to drink more than I should and daily. I was partying and I was working on making him feel what I felt, and it was not hard.

I met so many people working at the local gas station and I was quickly on my way to forgetting my vows to God and I started feeling myself and my desires.

I met men and I had fun but a feeling that I felt as a child came back up, I was curious again, I wanted to be with a woman.

This Man had me feeling empty, lost, and with little to no self-love. I thought about it so much, the enemy will happily help you offend and hurt God.

So as soon as I had the thought, the opportunity came up. I had a one-night stand with a woman and it was far from the fantasy I had in my mind. Another failure.

One thing that had always played in my mind was the love I had lost and the what if's. The thoughts were stronger than ever as I watched my life fall apart in front of my face.

I lost my job; my marriage was failing as it always was and not by my choice. My mother was heartbroken, her daughter who had been serving God side by side with her was now back in the streets.

I was constantly arguing with him and my mother in what seemed like an ongoing thing. My mother throughout the years maintained a relationship with her brother, my abuser, which always kept a gap between us. He was still at all family events and no one ever put a stop to it.

In the middle of my life crisis number, who knows which one, she had him come stay with us and visit from New York.

If I was going nuts that put me over the edge. I was a walking time bomb. I had to get out of there so I told my mom I was going to take a road trip to New Jersey. I needed to get away!

I heard the guy was released and so much time had passed and I was going back home to see if there was anything left.

My mother thought it was a great idea so I could drive her brother, my abuser back home. It's the audacity for me. I did it anyway.

I still remember all the things that played through my mind as I drove nineteen hours with my abuser and my three little girls in the car all the way home.

We made it back safely thank God and I finally got away from him. That situation made me so angry and so bitter, I was determined to find my lost love.

Only he could heal my heart, only he could make this pain go away. I found his older brother and asked where he was but he didn't know, so I gave him the telephone number where he could find me.

He called. He told me to come pick him up.

It was late at night when I pulled up on the block, Down Bottom on Union St.

He quickly came to the car and gave me the biggest hug! Nothing had happened between us. We were good.

He introduced me to what seemed like thirty people with so much love, especially from his big homey. Everyone looked up to him, everyone respected him but especially him.

He talked him up as if he was a movie star. I was honored to meet him. Many years would pass before I would bump into his big homey again.

We got into my car and drove back to my cousin's house where we sat in the living room having a very deep conversation.

Talking about what happened, that I had two more kids, his time locked up, and lastly that he still wanted to be with me.

He wanted me to stay and he gave me an ultimatum to leave my husband, the pain, the drama and start a new life with him.

He begged me, told me he would make me happy not to be scared and pulled out a stack of money and told me he would get me a place right then and help me raise the girls just do not leave him again.

I was so confused and scared I told him I could not, I could not leave my mom and all I had accomplished was to come back home. I broke his heart; I broke my heart.

At that moment all I could think about was God, all I had been brought up to believe. How could God bless me if I left the marriage, even though he was far gone from the marriage.

I tried to make sense of it and told him to give me time, I had to go back and fix things. My mother was waiting for me to come back, she constantly called me to ask when I was leaving.

He got up, he looked at me in my soul and said he loved me, that he would always love me but he was not waiting anymore he walked out and we did not even say goodbye.

I cried like a baby and even stayed a few days longer to see if he would come back, he didn't.

My mother popped up on me, she knew me and knew he had my heart and that I was crazy enough to leave everything and stay with the man I loved, the only one I had genuinely loved, the only one who NEVER hurt me.

We drove back to Georgia.

Me with a broken heart and a soul full of regret. Once again, I let love slip by me. Something I would heavily regret for the rest of my life.

Chapter Seven

I was back in Georgia, back to the cold lonely nights, the emptiness, and the partying. My husband and I were both doing whatever we wanted, when we wanted to, and with whoever we wanted to. Many times, for me I know it was nothing but late club nights, early mornings at Krystals for some small burgers, and crawling into bed with my babies.

I wasn't innocent, but I wasn't as bad as he made me out to be. I was just running away from my reality; I was a functional alcoholic.

I had a corporate office job by day, mother in the evening, and clubs almost every day of the week in the nightlife of Atlanta.

Atlanta was lit, Velvet Room, Room 112, and many others had ATL the place to be at one of the lowest emotional points of my life.

After seeing my guy, I was more convinced that I have been fooling myself into believing that being in this marriage was what God wanted for me.

I could not keep doing this, but I was not ready to go either. My brother was living with us for a while and he witnessed firsthand my roller coaster. He sat me down one day and looked at me and said "It's so easy to get lost, but it is so hard to find yourself once you're lost" . Those words touched my soul.

I was that person he was talking about. I was completely lost and would be lost for an exceedingly long time.

Like every other time that I wanted to try and save my marriage it was time to relocate.

So, we packed up, my brother and my husband drove the 24 ft U-Haul truck while I drove with my mom, a friend who needed a ride to Dallas, and the kids in front.

Just like my life this turned out to be one hell of a ride.

First, we got lost, we drove ten hours the wrong way and ended up in Houston, Mississippi. So, we had to drive ten hours the right direction before we even started heading to Texas! As if that wasn't bad, we were hauling a car attached to this massive truck and we got stuck in a gas station.

After about a good hour we were finally back on the road, where we got pulled over and of course my brother had no license. Let me just say that was the fastest I ever changed seats with someone.

We got away with that just to break down on the road and had to wait all night for someone to come fix the truck.

As you can imagine the stress levels were extremely high, my brother and I tried to find humor in the disaster road trip, but that quickly became impossible.

My husband and I had a huge fight in the middle of Mississippi. Police came out and thankfully let us go, but that was a very tense drive to Texas.

As soon as we arrived, he got on Greyhound and went to Louisiana. I was not mad at all to be honest. I was completely tired of him and his drama, cheating, lies, and disrespect.

I could not take a minute more of it, especially when I had just walked away from the love of my life to do right by a man who couldn't see me if you dressed me as a clown and had me perform. He only loved himself and the streets.

We had just arrived, and my mom asked me to drive her friend to Dallas and I did. I drove her there and drove back to Houston alone. I needed that four-hour drive home alone. I needed to think, what was I going to do now?

I needed to get my life together and now that my biggest distraction was gone it would be a perfect time to focus on my kids and provide for them.

I ended up getting hired at the U-Haul when I went to drop off the equipment. I never wasted time, one thing about me I was going to provide for my kids.

I was all they had, and thankfully my mother who was helping me take care of them so I could work. I always enjoyed working, I had been working since I was nine. I would answer the phones for my parent's cab company, and I loved it. "White Angels, where are you? Where are you going? ten minutes" I could do it in my sleep.

I got hired to rent trucks, but they quickly realized I was no ordinary girl, I was into everything, they could not keep in the office.

I was hooking up trailers, moving all the trucks, and quickly I was under cars installing hitches. It was hilarious to see men's faces when my boss would tell them I was installing their hitch.

My boss and I would get a kick out of their reaction every time, we were so cool. He took me under his wing and taught me like a big brother everything about installing hitches and everything U-haul he turned me into a beast.

We would smoke joints when no customers were around and listen to Tupac. He was older so he would also school me about life. Lessons I would carry forever.

My daughters were growing fast, my oldest was now five years old and starting kindergarten. I was loving my job, I loved getting dirty with the boys, but I needed more.

I enrolled in school to become a medical assistant, I always wanted to be in the medical field and now seemed like the perfect time.

Especially with my brother on top of me, pushing me to follow my dreams, finally I was focused.

We had a "field trip" early in the class to the Houston Forensics Center. That class escalated fast and we went from medical terminology to a real-life autopsy.

I was standing at the head of the patient watching as the medical examiner opened the man's skull and pulled his brain right out. It's crazy how there is nothing in this head but a brain and empty space it is quite incredible to see.

We all watched as he pulled out his tongue that he would cut into pieces for toxicology purposes. One by one we saw his organs.

The lungs really hit me hard, they were black due to smoking and as a smoker I saw firsthand what it does to you. It did not stop me though.

We left to see other bodies and we even saw a baby that was found in a basket. It broke my heart, but you gotta be professional and stay strong, something I was an expert at.

They took us to the John/Jane Doe room where bones just laid, they had never been claimed. We ended the tour watching them stuff garbage bags with the patient's organs back into the bodies and do a quick sew before they go to the funeral homes.

We walked out and I could taste the dead bodies in my mouth. The smell of decomposing bodies is so strong you can actually taste it, and it takes so long to go away.

I could only eat salads for a week after that the sight of meat reminded me of the human body and I could not get near it for at least a week.

I would do it all over again, that was one of the most educating experiences I have ever had in my life.

Most people can't say they have watched an autopsy performed in real life, but I was blessed to experience it.

It gave me the opportunity to see God's work firsthand, I always get a tickle out of people who do not believe in God, how else can you explain every organ perfectly housed inside this extraordinary body.

Even though I can understand why some feel that way and do not believe in God especially with the events that would soon follow that day.

First, Tropical Storm Allison devastated southeast Texas in June of 2001 the worst flooding that had occurred in Houston, where 30,000 became homeless after the storm flooded over 70,000 houses and destroyed 2,744 homes.

My house was one of those houses that flooded. My brother, my mother, and I carried my three daughters all night long as the water continued to come in. I saw God when the water stopped when it reached the sofa we were sitting on. A boat got us out the next day, then we walked to the nearest hotel.

Seemed like there were crowds in the streets, everyone was flooded, houses, cars. It was a scene from a movie except we were living it.

We would have to live in horrendous conditions while our house was gutted and fixed, we had nowhere to go.

In my desperation I trusted God. I continued to work and go to school even though my car flooded, even though we had to use the bathroom in buckets, even though I could not see light I continued to push forward.

September 11, 2001, we were sitting in class like any other day when the calls started coming in. There was a terrorist attack against the United States, planes crashed into the world trade center in New York that was just the beginning of a series of attacks where thousands lost their lives.

We sat and watched the news in class in despair as another plane crashed into the world trade center and we watched them collapse.

The United States had been compromised. I remember how scared we all felt. I left school and ran to my daughter's school to pick her up.

I went home and just hugged my babies, my heart hurting from the thought of so many never getting that opportunity again.

I can imagine how many people stop believing in God because of this tragedy, it did the opposite for me!

It made me believe more, trust more, have more faith, but most importantly it made me pray. 9-11, as the world would come to know this horrific day, not only shook the world but it also shook my life.

My husband decided he wanted to come back again and after all my brother had done to help my mother and I in the middle of all the occurrences I should have just sent him packing.

He had abandoned us, and it was my brother who saved us when we had no one, where would my mother and I be in that storm with them babies?

I was young and dumb I went against my mother, my brother, and reason.

I allowed this man back and I did not care who I would hurt, what the consequences would be, or how I would destroy all I have worked for once again for this man, who had absolutely nothing to offer me.

I still wanted to make my marriage work and I wanted my daughters to have their father.

I wanted to live right by God.

My brother was so upset with me because he had witnessed firsthand what I had gone through with my husband, and he did not want me to go backwards after coming so far.

He wasn't going to stand around and watch so he left. He ended up back in Trenton the hell he was running from, a place that only meant pain, depression, addiction, and what he warned me about the way to losing oneself. He quickly lost himself.

I had no idea at the time how my decisions would not only affect me but also the people I loved the most.

Here we were, "trying" again.

 I was already seeing my brother's warnings happening. I quit school, something he begged me not to do, but I did.

 It was not long before the fighting started again, I think this time it was more serious than previous ones.

 I regretted allowing him to come back immediately, I was doing amazing. Why did I go backwards?

I had given my phone number out at work prior to him moving back and that person called and asked for me. A fight broke out and things escalated quickly, he felt like I was playing him, and he grabbed two knives. He put one to my neck and one to his, as he pinned me to the wall.

 I remember my daughters crying and my mother begging him to stop.

My mother instinct kicked in and I blacked out, I grabbed him by the neck with both hands and all I knew when I came to, my mother was screaming "he is blue, let go, you're going to kill him!!!"

 He was blue. I let go quickly and he began to cough, when he got himself together, he looked at me and said "You're a crazy bitch!" And walked out.

I later realized he stole my Jay Z concert tickets; I was 38 hot!

He never came back, that was the last draw. It was like we both realized either he was going to kill me, or I was going to kill him, so it was time to get out and we finally did.

That would be the end of our eleven-year toxic relationship. The last time my daughters would see their father for years to come.

I continued to work at U-Haul even though I was down, I knew how to put my poker face on, and I was a pro at pretending to be okay.

I rented a truck to this guy, and he caught my attention because he looked like Jay Z and I loved Jay Z.

That started a conversation that turned into a date and quickly we were living together. It was just me being dumb as usual. It's so sad when you do not love yourself, because you walk around looking for love in all the wrong places.

 Looking back, I can see why I made that choice because he was different from anything I knew; he had a real job, a good one too.

He was older and was incredibly wise for his years since he had done Federal time and had changed his life around. Still the traits of that old life were very visible.

 I enjoyed our conversations because I was learning something, and knowledge has always been a turn on for me. I could not have been happier; I was finally becoming a better woman and we looked like we were building an empire together.

Then things started changing when we moved into an apartment together. I noticed that his old school ways were more than I wanted for my children.

I understood his logic, but it was not going to work for me and mines, he believed the children were not to sit in the living room and that is understandable when you have a mansion but not in a small two-bedroom apartment that would mean my girls would have to be in their bedroom all the time and that was not going to fly with me.

 That quickly became a major issue, his way of raising children did not match my relationship with my daughters because through all my difficulties they were always with me and to me they were not going to continue to suffer because of me.

 I was determined to stand up for them and do whatever I had to do to make sure that they knew that I had their backs.

 His kids came to visit from New York, and I was happy, coming from a toxic family. I love children and always had a way with them.

I embraced them immediately but quickly I noticed that my children were in their room like always and his, were in the bedroom with us. It was Christmas time, and he knew that due to my past I did not celebrate it.

We went out to buy gifts for his children and it was the night before Christmas, and we had to go to Walgreens because our financial situation was not the best at the time.

We got there and I immediately assumed that he was going to get all five of the kid's gifts and that was the moment of impact for me, he did not.

He came up with the "You don't celebrate Christmas" excuse and that was not okay with me. The way my brain and heart are set up I would not care who doesn't celebrate what, if I bought for one, I bought for all.

That day broke my heart and I went to his sister to vent thinking she would understand how I was feeling and the fact that my children were being treated indifferently, and instead of her helping she made it so bad. Next thing you know he is questioning my loyalty and all my motives. How did this happen?

He worked the early morning shift, and we were up around four AM arguing about the situation and during the argument he slapped me in my face, he said he tapped me I say you slapped me.

He apologized and tried to make it sound good, but my mind was made up, it was time to come up with a master plan but staying in the situation was not going to be an option for me and my babies.

I called my mom to come by that day while he was at work, and we sat at the kitchen table for a talk.

Our relationship was just starting to heal from the last argument we had a few months before when she asked me a question and I responded rudely "Who am I the mailman?"

I saw the look on her face, and I had not seen that look since I was a teenager and I quickly ran into the bathroom where my three daughters were bathing thinking she would not, she did. My mother came into that bathroom and hit me like I was still a young girl in her house, right in front of my daughters. They watched from the tub; I am not sure if they remember that, but I couldn't help but to wonder if they lost respect for me that day.

I was so hurt, but like always I quickly got over it and forgave her.

Our relationship continued because no matter what my mother had always been there for me and nothing she could ever do would change the love and admiration I had for her.

She proved why it was so easy to love her that afternoon as I told her how bad things were going and how my girls were getting treated.

My mother responded "So what do you want to do? " I knew what she meant, when were we leaving and where were we going?

One thing my mother did not play about was my daughters, she adores her granddaughters, and she would do anything and everything to protect them.

We figured out our funds and quickly realized we did not have enough money to rent a truck and get to the only place we could go, back home, back to Trenton.

I have always been a quick thinker so I came up with a plan. I told my mother I was going to rent a U-Haul truck locally which would only cost us a hundred dollars and we would take the truck to Trenton, and deal with the consequences later.

My mother was my rider and about them girls she was with it. I went down to my old job because I was no longer working at the time. I had actually taken the exam to become a corrections officer and passed. I was offered a job and was about to begin my new career when that slap changed my future.

I went in and spoke to one of my old coworkers and explained my plan to him, so he made sure he got me a brand-new truck and wished me well.

He was my angel. I knew God had sent him since he could have easily told or not agreed to help me, but instead he went above and beyond to get me out of there safely.

I took the truck to my sister's house and parked it across the street in the school parking lot and drove home to wait for him to come from work.

When he arrived, he looked like he felt bad for touching my face and I pretended to believe him and acted like everything was okay.

I had two cars, a nice Toyota Camry and what we called a "Hoopty", a Honda Accord that was only good for local use.

This man was so controlling he was riding in my nice car and had me and my girls riding in my Honda that was falling apart. I was tired and I was going to get out.

I had never been more determined in my life. I could see that knife to my neck, me choking this man until he was purple, the dead people on the autopsy tables, the flood, September 11th, and I reached a breaking point!

I told him I had to use the Camry the next day and that I would drop him off at work, whatever reason I gave, worked.

The next morning just like the day before when he slapped me, we were up at four AM but this time I was dropping him off. What he did not know was it would be the last time he would see me.

He said bye to me very nonchalant as if he would see me for dinner.

I just watched as he walked away knowing that would be the last time, we were not the same.

I sat in the parking lot for a few minutes crying, thinking of all the good times we shared, of our deep talks, and all the things he had taught me that I would take with me forever.

He was truly an amazing man, and if I were a single woman, I believe we could have done big things, but as a mother of three I knew he was not the man for me.

I put the car in reverse and flew home to pack and get out of there before two o'clock when he would be back. My mother was ready, she helped pack the house and quickly grab all my things, while my sister and I loaded the truck quickly.

You never know how strong you are until you must carry all your furniture from the second floor with your sister.

That was the normal in my life though, I was a young girl steaming walls to remove wallpaper for my mom to save on labor. I would watch my father for hours fixing cars, anything from a tune up to installing a new motor.

It was amazing to see how he lifted that car motor with that big machine, looking back it was a whole forklift haha.

I learned so many things from my father and I loved him for it.

Although he abandoned our home, he made me into a little man to take care of the home he left behind. I am good with tools; I can put things together as well as take them apart kind of how I was in my own life.

It was time to go, I would drive the truck and my mother would follow with my three babies in the car. That worked for me because I could smoke the whole way and think about my life, figure out how I got to this place to this moment and what would I do now?

I was thinking about saying goodbye to my sister, that was very emotional for me.

I hated that I was leaving her behind alone in Texas, but I felt completely alone the whole time I lived there.

 My sister and I love each other very much and I don't ever question that, but our way of thinking is completely different.

 I respect her more than I could ever express. She is strong, hardworking, clean, and she loves very hard.

 Unfortunately, we bumped heads too often and in our stubbornness we did not value and appreciate the time together. It is still sad thinking about it today.

As I write this a tear comes to my eyes knowing that today we have no relationship, my sister as well as my mother are both Jehovah's witnesses and as you will continue to read, my life choices have stopped them from talking to me.

What that means is they do not speak to me and have not for a very long time.

We speak sporadically if something is wrong with our mother, but I basically have no relationship with them today.

 One of God's creations that I love is the brain, another fact that God exists is memory.

The fact that we can store memories like files, and we can pull them out when needed not only shows the intelligence that was needed to create us but the love that he has for us.

I have so many wonderful memories with my sister and my mother and the fact that they don't talk to me because they want to please the loving father that we all serve is respectable to me.

I love that they love God more than me, I love that they are willing to sacrifice everything for their love of our father.

Who can be mad at that? Not me.

I love them and I know one day God will clarify whatever needs to be clarified until then I keep them in my prayers as I know they keep me in theirs. That is true love.

I was basically homeless; I had no home, nowhere to go and a U-Haul full of stuff and I was full of emotions.

I had stolen the truck so I was anxious about what I would say when I got there, especially when I did not have the money to pay for it.

We were on the road, and I was on full overload, I am surprised I could focus on the GPS. I was so overwhelmed I became sick, halfway to Jersey.

At the gas station I told my mom to check me because I was not feeling good, and she told me I was burning up.

I had a fever and that was not going to stop me. I grabbed some fever reliever and kept driving.

We stopped at a hotel in Virginia because I was not getting any better, I had a high fever and needed to rest.

The next morning, we drove to Trenton, and I was in the emergency room. I had walking pneumonia and was lucky to have made the drive thirty-two hours running a high fever.

My mother, kids, and I went to my father's house where my cousin, and he opened the doors and allowed us to stay. I was so grateful.

I prayed the whole way to go drop off the truck and of course God was on time and showed up like always, they heard my story and did not charge me a dime!

I did not know anything about praise dancing back then because if I did it would have been a hallelujah praise dancing time up in there.

I was so thankful I went back to my dad's house to recover from my illness.

I was upstairs in the attic resting, so I could figure things out. I needed to quickly get a job and get us somewhere to live.

 I also knew the system and I was not too proud to get help for us if it came to that, I just needed to get my health in order so I could figure things out.

I went downstairs to get something to drink, and my heart was full, walking through the house I grew up in I felt at home.

 I was taken back to the growth in our family, how we could come so far that they would help us in our time of need. I knew that things were bad but at least for the first time since I was four years old my family was together again and that was all that mattered.

If you have not noticed, things change quickly in my life so you must pay attention.

 I walked into the kitchen to get a drink and what I got was my bubble popped.

 My father's wife and he were arguing, she was leaving, she said, she told my dad that she would go stay in a hotel until we left.

I was crushed, honestly that truly broke my heart.

 I walked in, their look of shock when they realized I heard them was priceless, and I for the first time was able to stay calm.

 That for me was growth. I normally would go ham, I would curse her out from A to Z, ready to fight and all, but today, I did not care.

Now I had been through too much, I was so beat up from life, I had no fight. Plus, I was a mother now and I did not want my siblings to feel like I was disrespecting their mom because this was a pattern.

She started and I finished, and I was always the bad guy because I turned all the way up.

This time I would walk away gracefully. I told my cousin, "You don't have to leave; this is your house we will leave."

I went upstairs and got my poor mother who was just sitting on the bed looking worried about my health and told her we had to go to grab our things.

My mother and I have always had a deep connection and with one look and one let's go she did not ask any questions! My ride or die grabbed our things and jumped in the car and drove around the corner to my sister's house.

I still remember the sadness in my father's eyes. What could he do?

I try not to think about what he could do because I only hurt myself. I rather remember the look in his eyes because in that look I saw how much he loved me and how it hurt him as he stood there watching my mother, kids, and I driving off.

Not knowing where we would go or what we would do. That was hard for us too.

My sister let us stay immediately. It felt good, being with my sister again after so many years apart, she has always been my favorite, she taught me everything from bathing to fighting back. My sister and I had been through many things together. Our relationship is something you cannot explain, we are deeply connected.

It was so bad that when she gave birth to my nephew, she did not call anyone to say she was in the hospital, but our connection or maybe it was the holy spirit that told me, either way I showed up at her house when the neighbors told me she went to give birth.

I remember walking into her hospital room as she sat there alone staring at our baby boy. Her eyes lit up when she saw me, she asked how I knew she was there, and I told her your heart called me.

That was a moment we would hold very dear to our hearts. That would be the case with all her children. I would show up every time. We are spiritual beings; the holy spirit is always at work connecting us with those we love.

I was sitting on my sister's porch just trying to breathe for a minute, overwhelmed with all I was going through, and my sister was always busy.

Mother of five children she was cooking, cleaning, doing laundry, running after my nieces and nephews who are the love of my life.

I would run her ears with everything going on and she would just listen to my stories. Something she still enjoys. I have always had a story to tell but in reality, it is not a story it is my life.

My brother, the one who left Texas just a few months earlier was there also, and it was then when I realized how my mistakes do not only affect me but also those around me.

My brother came back home because of my wrong decision and found himself at rock bottom, exactly where I was standing homeless, nowhere to go, LOST, and he turned back to his old coping mechanism, addiction.

It was a slap to my face to see him that way, and I was just living my life. If my situation would not have changed and put me where I was now side by side homeless with him, I would not have known or could ever understand the extent of my damage.

I love rock bottoms; they are lessons in rock bottoms that you could never learn in mountain tops.

I tried talking to him but at that point even though he never acted indifferent with me, or ever made me feel bad he did not have to.

The reality of where we were spoke more volume than any words could ever.

He told me he loved me every day before leaving to do what he did in the streets. He always used the same sentence for all of us "love you, big bunch, damn straight, clown sucker jaws" something we will carry for all eternity.

I was sitting there full of guilt.

It was all my fault; my brother was on the streets in these places doing these things because of a decision that I made.

This man was in Texas, ten stacks in his pocket, a nice car, a job, and doing everything to help my mom and me. I was in school about to be a medical assistant and I chose to go back to a man that would do what he always did to destroy me.

This time he did not only destroy me, but this time it destroyed my brother too and I was sick. I would wait until he came back to my sister's house, and I would lay on the floor with him as he had the shakes and hold him praying to God to forgive me for looking at what my life choices had done.

I was responsible for someone else's hurt and I hated how that felt. I hated the fact that we were there, but there we were. Homeless, on our sisters living room floor, our mother on the sofa, all our kids upstairs, but at that moment we were all together.

For the first time in what seemed like forever my mother and her three kids were all together and you could always smell the love in the kitchen because one thing about us, we can cook.

This felt good, watching my kids play with their cousins was priceless. Every time my nephew would run by, he already knew the drill he gotta come give me my love!

I needed my hug, and I would kiss him to death he knew then, and he knows now he's my boy. That is my son. He made me a mother for the first time, ever since he was born, I knew what it felt like to love someone more than you love yourself.

There is nothing I would not do to protect him. My nieces were my first daughters, they are my heart. The love these girls show me till this day is so overwhelming that it brings me to tears, every time I get the chance, I thank them for loving me. That kind of love for me is beyond rare.

I was trying to put everything I had just endured behind me and just enjoy watching our kids' bond and play like I had never left.

Being gone for so long my children had missed being raised with their cousins like I had growing up. My cousins are an especially important part of my life, it was like having extra sisters and brothers. My cousins and I share so many special moments and I had robbed my kids from that being so far.

I was grateful for the tough times since they brought my children back to family and watching them play made me forget all I was going through.

I was just feeling better. A few days had passed and I was thankfully recovering well, so my sister and I decided to go for a drive. A drive that would change my life and those around me.

We turned on Third St where we quickly saw our friend who also happened to be the sister of my love, yes, the one I had walked away from five years before.

I had heard he had recently had a baby and I did not even want to disturb his life because I knew our bond was still there because he was still on my mind and life had taught me early on when someone is on your mind that it is heavy because you are on theirs.

We pulled over to say hi since we had been friends since childhood, we were even in the same class as children so I could not ride by my girl and not say hi.

Immediately it was all love. We were so happy to see each other, and she quickly brought up her brother and how he was going to lose it when he found out I was back in the town.

I remember like it was yesterday that I quickly told her "Please don't tell your brother I am here! I don't want to cause him any problems and you know if he knows I am here it will be a problem."

We laughed casually because she knew as much as I that our love had overcome separation and time. Our love was alive then as it had been all of them years ago. I could feel it.

We continued to talk when in the background I heard a voice say, "Who is that?" and her cousin responded ``don't even look that way, that is your brother right there, he quickly responded "My brother can't handle that like me!"

I was taken back.

I asked my girl who it was and she quickly said girl that is my baby brother do not pay him no mind and sent him inside.

We laughed and we left even though she told me her brother was on vacation in Florida. I did not want to hang around something inside of me kept telling me to stay away and not to come back around.

I told my sister that I did not want him to know I was around, that I was not there to bring problems to him or to myself, I was over drama, and I knew that seeing him would cause drama.

 I was still thinking up to that point, nothing I had been through could compare to what I was getting ready to endure.

 That feeling I was having was the holy spirit speaking to me. I was clearly hearing God speak to me telling me to move forward! Not to look back at what could have been, because he was now a father of a five-month-old baby and that was all that mattered to me!

I loved him enough to let him go and I was not going to waiver.

I went back to my sister's house and continued to focus on a master plan. I had to find work and I needed to find my mother and I a home. I had no time to waste.

I had arrived in Trenton Sunday and now it was Sunday a week to the day when I woke up feeling very peaceful, so I went and sat down on the front porch, something I always do even today.

 I was in deep thought when my niece came running out with the house phone saying it was for me. I asked who it was, and she said it was my friend, his sister, my heart dropped. She did not listen, I thought to myself, and I knew that when I said hello, he would be on the other side of the phone, and I was right.

Chapter 8

Sweating, I answered the phone with a nervous hello, my girl quickly said somebody wants to talk to you, my heart sank.

He got on the phone, and he lost it. He was so excited that I was there and around the corner that he didn't say much on the phone besides, "where are you at?"

Once I said my sister's house, he said I'm coming I'll be right there, I didn't even get the chance to say anything he hung up!

I can only imagine him running into the car! He got there so fast. I was a hot mess; hair was not done. I had barely woken up and before I could even run the brush through my hair, he was outside beeping the horn.

I was sweating, shaking, a hot mess and he was downstairs.

There was no time for any of that. After five years I would finally see the love of my life and even more importantly I wasn't leaving.

I was home and all those feelings I had went out the window.

I ran downstairs and there he was smiling from ear to ear. I hugged him for what seemed like forever. We were safe in each other's arms and without speaking any words we missed each other more than we could say.

He ran to the car and got the picture of his baby girl and was proudly showing her off.

He was so excited about being a father and he was determined to be the best father in the world and for me that was everything!

Especially since my husband hadn't looked back to my daughters.

We spoke briefly and he was so hyped he told me he was going to get a haircut and that he would be right back, not to go anywhere. I smiled and said OKAY.

He walked towards his car and turned back around, and kissed me on my cheek, afterwards he said, "Don't talk to any guys either, don't even think about getting involved because you are still mine!"

I smiled from ear to ear, and he quickly made it known he was serious when he sternly said, "I'm not playing" I responded with a "I know" and off he went.

I was cooking that day so I hurried to clean up and get things ready so that I could get to it.

I always play Spanish music when I am cooking so I was in my zone,

I was dancing in the fridge looking for my ingredients when I turned around for a quick turn, yes, I was getting it.

I noticed he was standing there watching. How long had he been watching me dance alone in the kitchen, how embarrassing I thought?

He smiled and quickly snatched me up and just gave me a passionate kiss. It had been such a long time and I could not say no.

It had been so many years since we kissed for five years. I had last seen him that last time about two years prior, but we did not kiss that time.

We both knew it was over. We wanted to be together for five years of trying to get back to each other and now seemed like it may be the time.

I forgot about everything at that moment, especially the voice that was telling me to stay away. After a few more kisses he told me he had to go but that he wanted me to get showered and dressed so that he would be back around seven to pick me up.

I was surprised because we never did that, go out and do anything. Our relationship was not normal; we had to hide most of it.

Not that this was any different because he still was living with the mother of his child. He said he was going to go home and get showered and ready and he would be back, I said okay still ignoring the voice in my head.

I was like a teenage girl getting ready for prom. I had on a burgundy body shirt with some blue jeans. I wanted to look sexy but still classy.

I was finishing the last few touches when like clockwork he appeared on time he was early.

He was so happy to see me all glammed up and he showed his admiration. We headed out and we decided to leave his car and take mine.

We were walking to the car when his little brother walked by, the same one who was talking about how he could handle me better, and he said to him "Don't do nothing I wouldn't do." They laughed, and he told him to go home, and he loved him, and he said he loved him too.

We got in the car and started cruising through the town. We drove through all sides of Trenton stopping at the corner store, everywhere we went they showed him love so he was showing love back.

We were driving when he just stopped the car, put the music down and said we need to talk, he was so serious.

He asked me if my middle daughter was his?

I was taken back and quickly said no not at all she actually looks just like her father, and he would not accept that, I even said "that girl is white with blue eyes, do you see how dark we are?" He responded saying there were white Puerto Ricans with blue eyes in his family.

I just continued to tell him she was not his daughter and there were no possibilities of her being anyone else's but my husband.

He looked at me with the most serious look and said "I know that's my daughter and I will take that to my grave" he turned the music up and continued driving. I knew he was wrong, and I tried to tell him but there was no convincing him of the truth, he wanted her to be his and in his mind she was.

We drove through Down Bottom. He was looking for his cousin, he wanted to see his cousin so bad we were driving everywhere looking for him, but we never found him that night.

He jumped out of the car a few times and was hugging his friends and showing mad love. It was a beautiful sight.

He got back in the car and told me he was done driving around looking for his cousin, that now we needed to have a serious talk and I was thinking about another one, this guy is on a roll.

We drove to Third Street Park and parked on the dark side, and he started spilling his heart to me. He told me he loved me, that he always loved me, that things were not good at home and that he was tired of just living life without me. That it was time for us to finally be together and stop worrying about how other people felt.

He reminded me how hurt we had been in the last five years not being able to be together. He showed me his new tats, I showed him mine, and we made a deal that we would get matching tats and cover ups since we both had someone else on us.

He promised me that he was going to help me get a place and get out of my sister's house and that this would be the last time that I would suffer.

He promised that he was going to make me happy and that all my sufferings were about to end. I looked at him and told him "I did not come here to break up a happy home" and he looked at me and said you cannot break something that is already broken.

It was our time he said and that was it, I had never seen him more determined. I had denied him before, but I was not about to deny him this time.

I agreed, we hugged and kissed, and things started getting hot in the car, so we decided to drive around the corner to a more secluded location.

We had nowhere to go so we made love in the car, we made love that night like it would be our last time, little did I know it would be.

We stayed in that spot for a long time just loving each other, we said how much we loved and missed each other, and nothing was left unsaid.

It was getting late and although we had our future planned, he still had to go home and be a responsible man.

We knew these things would take time if we were going to do it the right way and try to avoid drama.

Instead of going back to my sister's house we went the opposite direction, he wanted to see if he saw his cousin again.

We were driving up Stokely when a car drove by slowly and he was also driving slowly, it seemed like they were both trying to see who the other person was.

I was so naive looking back, I did not think anything of it.

I was on cloud nine. I was finally going to be happy with the guy I loved. He stopped the car, and I was confused, he told me to hold on, he was going to talk to this guy. The music was playing, he walked behind the car to talk with the guy, I saw no problem.

He came back to me and said jump into the driver's side which I found strange, but I figured he did not want to drive anymore so I did.

I put my seat belt on, my glasses on. I was ready when he was, but he was still talking.

He came back again but this time his tone had changed, he said he was going to fight the boy really quick and my neck nearly broke looking at him like he was crazy!

I quickly responded, "No you're not, you just told me how much you changed, about your daughter, and our future so get in the car and let's go!"

I still remember the look he gave; it was like he was thinking your right and that is why I love you; he knew I kept him balanced. I always wanted him to do the right thing and he knew that.

He started walking backwards and said your right and was about to get in the car when the guy pulled out a gun.

He pointed the gun at him, and I just remember putting my glasses down and begging for his life!

I pleaded with that guy. I told him he has a daughter please don't do this, I begged and begged, and he pulled the trigger.

My guy fell sitting down and I just stood in shock as the guy turned and looked at me with the gun in his hand. I knew the street rules and you do not leave any witnesses behind, so I figured I was next.

He looked at me and it looked like he was getting ready to take me out but then something changed, his eyes opened up so big. It was like he saw a ghost and just ran.

I still wonder what it was he saw; my faith tells me he saw an angel, whatever he saw did not allow him to hurt me.

I ran out of the car and grabbed my guy trying to get him in the car, and he just said call the police, we did not have cellphones and we were in the middle of the street.

I did not know what to do. I could not move him, I tried and tried, and just could not, he had lost consciousness and I began screaming for help.

I yelled and yelled for help as I just laid on his chest crying begging him not to leave me. How could he do this to me? He promised me we were going to be together. How could he do this to me?

I saw some kids on bikes and even though I knew CPR at that moment I did not know anything! I asked them to do CPR, they were kids you can imagine the desperation I was feeling.

I could not move, I was helpless, he was dying in my arms, and I could not do anything.

Someone must have heard me when the police and ambulance arrived and quickly threw me in the back of the police car and that would be the beginning of a nightmare.

The police took me to the police station, they had me there asking me questions all night. I kept asking when can I go? I needed to get to the hospital, I needed to go see him.

They were not telling me anything at all, just questioning me.

I was traumatized, I was sitting there with his blood on my clothes and the events playing in my head repeatedly, what if I would have done this, what if I would have done that?

Still no clarity.

After being interrogated all night suddenly the detective's phone rings, he just yells out "This just became a homicide investigation!!!" and that was how I found out that the love of my life was gone. I just cried and cried and cried.

They took me back to my sister's house because I was so upset that I was of no use to anyone after that call.

I sat in the back of the detective's car crying it seemed like the longest ride I had ever been on knowing my life could never be the same again!

That didn't matter, all I could think about was his daughter! The fact that she no longer had her daddy, the most amazing father anyone could ask for and she would never get the chance to see it for herself.

I was broken, the guilt was overwhelming, and it became worse when we pulled up to my sister's house and his car was still parked out front.

Why didn't I listen to the voice that told me to stay away?

Now there was a family in pain; they lost a son, a brother, and a father! Sadly, I knew his family. His sister was one of my best friends. How could I face her?

How could I look them in their faces knowing it was me he was with?

That day my family did not say much, they knew I was devastated, and I am sure they had never seen that look on my face before.

To make matters worse it was March 25th my daughter's birthday, the same one he took to his grave with him.

Instead of me celebrating my daughter's birthday I was grieving!

I was walking to the corner store when I noticed his sister and aunt walking towards me, I immediately felt sick to my stomach the moment I was dreading.

They asked me what happened, and I told them and that is when his sister asked me not to come to the house to give his mother my condolences and to just stay away out of respect for his daughter's mother and of course I understood.

I also spoke to his baby's mother when she came to pick up the car he was driving and although it was wrong, I lied and said nothing happened.

I said that nothing was going on between us and I wanted to keep it that way. The last thing I wanted was to cause her more pain, other than the one she was already feeling.

We had a very respectful conversation and she even told me she would let me be a part of their daughter's life and I did not want to ruin that.

I had nothing but love for the baby, she was the love of his life. How could I not love her? I wanted nothing more than to be a part of her life.

After talking with the three of them I was exhausted emotionally, I still had not been to sleep but I continued to walk to the store.

I was almost at the store and I looked to the right and I thought I saw a ghost; my guy was walking towards me but how could that be he was gone! He was no longer with us!

I froze and my friend who was with me asked what was wrong? I said it is him she just grabbed me and said "no it's not that's his baby brother."

They had the same walk I could not move, I stood there until he came up.

This was the same guy from the first day in front of his house, and the same one from last night, now he was here in front of me asking what happened to his brother all I could do was cry.

I could not take it anymore, first his sister, aunt, then his girlfriend and now his brother and I just got out of the shower after removing the clothes I had on that had his blood all on them.

I just sat on the toilet hugging my clothes crying feeling like my heart was being ripped from inside of me and now I had to explain to another person what happened to their loved one.

I broke down, he just hugged me.

He just lost his brother and yet he was comforting me.

He walked me and my friend back to my sister's house and we sat outside on the porch, and I told him all that happened.

My daughters came out and I told him who they were, he asked where their father was, and I told him that he was in Louisiana, and I could see the sadness in his eyes like it touched him that my girls were fatherless.

The next day out of nowhere he returned and said he just wanted to check to make sure I was doing okay.

He also came to bring my daughters some candy. I was taken back as he handed me three black bags full of candy.

I really appreciated it because at that point I felt like the world was against me, the guilt was eating me alive, and I could not help but to feel so hurt that I was asked to stay away and not to even come to the burial.

I was devastated, I felt the world on top of me caving in. He knew all these things and wanted me to know that he did not feel that way!

He knew his brother loved me; he knew I was hurting like everyone else was. That meant a lot to me.

He told me that he would keep me informed about all the funeral arrangements so that at least I knew.

About two days later my sister sits me down with tears in her eyes and says to me that she is so sorry and that it hurt her to have to tell me, but her spouse wanted me to leave because I had witnessed that murder and word on the street was, I was in danger also.

Again, I put my mother and kids in the car, and we were back to being homeless.

We went around the corner to my aunt's house, and she agreed to let us stay in the downstairs apartment that my uncle used as his hang out.

My aunt lived in the top apartment, and my cousin lived in the front apartment.

It felt good. We were with our family, we had our own space and until I could figure things out this was exactly what we needed.

Things were so crazy for me it seemed like I was spiraling out of control so fast mentally, I could not think straight.

 I tried to get a job and I worked three days and had to quit; I could not handle it.

 I was getting in my car, playing the same songs repeatedly driving up and down all the streets that reminded me of him. I was out of it.

I started drinking immediately, I was trying to cope but I could not.

I had been through so much in such little time that I was completely lost. I think back to those days and I remember that my body was there, but I was not there.

His brother informed me of the date and time of the funeral, and of course I was not allowed to go but I could not accept that.

My loyalty to him would not allow me to walk away, we spent five years trying to only be together and love each other and this is where it ended.

I had to go and say goodbye. I called the funeral home and I explained who I was and all that was happening and by the grace of God they gave me permission to come before the family.

 Around three o 'clock my friend went with me to the funeral home so I could say see you later to my first love.

I walked into the empty funeral home where he laid dressed in baby blue, his favorite color.

 He looked so peaceful, like he was sleeping. I could not get close at first, I just sat in the middle and cried.

 My friend just sat there quietly crying because she lost a friend too, he was like a brother to her. We all grew up together.

This was a tremendous loss to so many, everyone loved him.

While we were driving around that night, he kept complimenting me on my watch, he loved it, so I took it off, put it in his pocket, and zippered it up.

I told him he could have it to take a piece of me with him.

I cried asking him why did he leave me when he knew I was alone in this world, what was I supposed to do?

Walking out of that funeral home knowing I would never see him again was the worst feeling I had ever had.

I was not the same person that walked in, I was dead too. I was a walking zombie, and I did not care about anything at all. I was just functioning.

That evening after the funeral his brother and sister came to my friend's house where I was, and we all cried, and it would be the last time that things between us would be as normal as could be.

Things changed very quickly. The next evening, I bumped into their older brother, and it was the first time we spoke since everything that happened. I hadn't seen him in years since the last time I was looking for his brother a few years before.

We spoke for a little and I told him what had happened and how we were looking for his cousin all night, so we jumped in my car and went to look for his cousin this time we found him.

We were smoking, drinking, and reminiscing about old days when we all used to hang in my apartment.

I told him we were looking for him all night and it was very emotional.

We were all drunk and high and we ended up in a hotel room.

I do not even understand what happened when I look back at that night, but his brother and I ended up having sex in the bathroom.

My body was there, mentally, and emotionally I was gone, I do not remember anything besides the fact that it happened.

I will never excuse what I did, I hated myself then and I hated myself for years after that night, a life full of regret.

We left and I quickly dropped him off and returned to my friends' house where I continued to drink.

I was drinking so heavily, I was not only running from the tragedy of losing my love but now I was living with the disgust that I betrayed him, that he was not even in the ground, and I had crossed him, I wanted to die.

I felt like the biggest trash and the worst part, I could not understand how I even got myself in that situation, there was nothing there.

No attraction, no flirting, nothing, it just happened.

It would be something that would haunt me for years.

We both acted like it never happened. I think we both felt the same way and a few days later he went to prison.

I was grateful that I would not have to see him and be reminded of the person I was.

I was trying to juggle being a mom in the day and heavily drinking all evening to the next morning and I was not letting up.

His younger brother was still coming by every day to check on us and to hang out.

I started to notice that he was a loner like me, he really did not have anyone to vent to or talk to and he felt bad for me because I was just a lost puppy in my car driving around in circles with no direction.

I had no desire to live, and he knew that so he would come around to make sure I stayed alive.

He did not even know that I was dealing with the guilt of what I had done with his brother and everything I was dealing with before all this happened.

I was baggage, heavy duty baggage and he was only seventeen proving to be the realest friend I had.

Seeing how he was always around me, people started making up lies and spreading gossip.

We were parked in front of my aunt's house talking and I was getting ready to go in the house. I was in my pajamas, I had just come out to chop it up with him really quick before I went to bed.

When out of nowhere, I heard yelling and it sounded familiar.

It was his sister; she was angry I could tell but I had no idea why.

She came up to me screaming and shouting accusations! It was not enough that I took her brother. Now I was trying to take the other one.

Now although I wanted to be understanding, I knew hurt people hurt people.

Then I realized hurt people hurt people and I also was hurt.

I was so angry because it was not true, I was not involved with him at all, nothing was going on and here I was getting disrespected in front of my aunt's house where my mom and kids were inside.

At that moment I blacked out and I just snapped.

I began to fight his sister.

I saw red and everything I was feeling inside I took it out on her.

Her brother and other people came and broke it up, picked her up and they all left. I went inside and immediately after laying down I knew that this would cost me.

It did, the next day my cousin came and let me have it. I disrespected my aunt's house. I had it coming, I was told to leave.

My mother and children were allowed to stay until I could find a place, but I had to go.

Just like that I was in my car homeless again.

This time I was not going to look for anywhere else to go. I just sat in my car in the cold wondering what I had done to deserve this life.

His baby brother showed up while I sat in front of my friend's house wondering what I would do next or in other words when would I get drunk again?

He apologized for what happened, especially when he knew there was absolutely nothing going on between us. He felt even worse when I told him I was kicked out behind what happened.

That night it was cold, I stayed in my car all night, turning it on and off so I could warm up and he sat in that car with me all night.

We talked. I told him all that happened, how I left Texas and how I had been kicked out three times in less than two weeks. I cried and he listened.

It was a long night, but I have to say I was so grateful to have him there in the midst of my rock bottom.

The next day after spending time with my girls and dropping them back at my aunts with my mother I met up with his brother, his friend, and my cousin.

We went to drop her off at her house when I decided to stop at 7-11 to grab cigarettes because we had a car full of liquor and we were going to get drunk like every other night since the tragedy.

I was standing in line waiting for the cashier and he was taking long, so I yelled out "Hey Pops I gotta go!"

Immediately the girl in front of me turns around and looks at me from head to toe with a dirty look and turns back around.

Me being who I am, I said to myself "Self! Let's ignore her, you're tripping, you didn't see that!" But I wanted to make sure I didn't make that up, so I said it again "Yo Pop's wassup I gotta go!"

Immediately she did it again.

I thought of all the liquor and weed in the car and decided it was in my best interest to walk away. So, I ignored her again, she left and I purchased my cigarettes, and I was immensely proud of myself.

That did not last long, I walked outside and started packing my cigarettes, but something told me to just stand in front of the camera.

The lady drives up and stops the car and just starts staring at me like I owe her money and at that point I could not take it.

I asked her in not so English what she was looking at?

She responded with some choice words, and it happened again I blacked out!

I walked up to the car and began beating her butt through the car window when I heard kids screaming!

This fool not only left her kids in the car all by themselves while she was in the store but second, she stopped the car to start a fight while them kids were in the car.

As much as I just wanted to stop and feel compassion, all I felt was anger for her putting her babies in that predicament!

I felt someone grabbing me and it was his brother who picked me up and put me in my car and we left! This lady began following us in her car and me being a hot head, I pulled the car over and jumped out.

The lady started driving fast towards me and was about to hit me with her car when he grabbed me and pulled me out the way saving my life, the car hit my leg.

I still have a small scar. It was not serious thanks to him grabbing me, that could've ended up very differently.

We got in the car and sped off, she tried following us, but I left her in the dust but not before she got my license plate number.

That night we got so drunk, I hit my tire on the curb and got a flat tire.

We ended up walking over the Trenton makes world takes bridge to get home it was a chilly night.

As we walked even though we had been drinking the adrenaline of the flat tire and the cold sober us up really quick.

We talked about so many things including my brother and the guilt I carried for him being out in the streets. We walked down the alley way I knew he would hang out at, and he helped me look for him in the abandoned houses.

I had been crying about him the whole walk. We found him and we talked for a while out in the cold! He just said what he always says to make me feel better "Love you, damn straight, clown sucker jaws"

It did not work!

That night I cried as we walked to my friend's house feeling like the world's biggest piece of trash.

I hated myself so much, couldn't anyone hate me more then I hated me.

No matter how bad people were talking about me which they did often, could not one dog me out more than I dogged myself out. Self-hatred is worse than any hate.

I appreciated how he not only helped me find my brother but also that he sat out there with me and made sure I got around the way to my friend's house safely.

This guy was loyal, and I was so grateful to have him.

For the next few days, we kept hanging, and people kept accusing us and talking about us when there was nothing at all going on.

We ignored them and got more drunk.

Here we were sitting around drinking and crying trying to cope with the loss of his brother and add the guilt I was carrying which he knew nothing about, nobody did.

I hated everything about my life but not as much as I hated me.

I drove him around to his house; I did not want to hang out that night.

My friend told me to stay at her house and so I wanted to go in early.

We were sober, I needed a break. I don't even know how I was surviving!

We sat there for a minute talking about everything that was going on. I was clearly terribly upset about it all.

I remember us being so mad about the accusations and him saying "The way we are being accused we might as well be doing it" and I agreed, it was like fighting to prove yourself and no matter how much evidence you show no one believes you.

We were laughing about it and just as we laughed, we looked at each other and just kissed.

It was so sincere.

There was no motive, no ill will, we had a passionate kiss and that was the scariest part about it.

This was no regular kiss, this was a kiss filled with emotions, energy, and it was not something I could not ignore.

After feeling completely dead and walking around like a zombie for over a month I felt something again. I did not know what it was, but it was something.

Chapter 9

I could not sleep that night, that short kiss did something to me and now people were going to really think they were right all along, but they were wrong.

 To the contrary the false judgement and accusations had pushed us to that point.

We were defending ourselves before this, I even fought his sister and was homeless because of these false accusations and it had been weeks after that.

I wanted to pack my kids and my things and run but for some reason I wanted to see him again, I wanted to talk about what happened and see where his head was.

I was terrified to lose him, in just over a month he became my best friend and the only person that was there with me at such a low point in my life.

He came by and nothing had changed between us except the way we were looking at each other.

There was something there that wasn't there before.

That night we became intimate, and I had never felt with anyone what I felt with him that night. The next day I knew I had to set matters straight, I could tell by the connection that this was serious, and it reminded me of how me and his late brother started.

 I was feeling real feelings and so was he.

I was scared, I did not want to hurt him, and there was something he did not know about me: the fact that I had a one-night stand with his brother and that I was carrying that around.

 We went to the third street park to hang out, something we did very often, since I had no place to live. It was our hang out.

I remember us sitting down talking but this time was different, we were acting like a couple, and I knew that if I wanted to have any chances, I had to say the truth, and I had to do it right then, so I did.

 I told him the truth about his brother and me.

It was one of the hardest truths I ever had to tell anyone, but I refused to lie to him when he had been nothing but loyal to me. I never regret telling him the truth that day.

He was not happy; he walked away from me and took a while to think alone, and I am assuming to take that news in.

After a while he came back and told me that although he was really pissed that he could not be mad at me because one I was not with him and second the fact that I told him such a big truth made him respect me and want to be around me more.

 That day we decided that we were going to be in a relationship and that he wanted to help me raise my daughters. He said he did not care what anyone had to say about me, that he knew me, and what I had been through.

He wanted to go through life with me. I was lost but I felt safe with him, so I was willing to try it.

Being six years older than him and a mother of three I had a lot going on in my world, and I did not have a clue about all he had been through and all the demons he was carrying not including the tragedy and the loss that connected us.

We were off to a rocky start.

I was homeless, did not have a home and not being able to be with my kid's full time was not going to work for me.

I went down to social services and asked for help. They immediately put me in a hotel, I quickly picked up my kids, and we went to the hotel.

It was rough knowing I had my kids in this situation because one thing about me was God kept a roof over my head and this was completely out of my comfort zone.

I did not understand back then but God will take you out of your comfort zone purposely to draw your attention back to him.

To remind you that without him you are nothing, and I needed to remember.

I was so far away from God; I had allowed my relationship with my husband to distract me and lose sight of what was important.

I had put a man before God, and before me.

Now I was completely emotionally beat up in a hotel with three small children and a new relationship with the brother of my first love.

I could not think I was just functioning.

I was trying to be as normal as possible and just be grateful that after being in the streets and from house to house for the last two months that I could just rest my head on a bed and watch tv while watching my kids play with my guy who was a natural father at only seventeen.

Since the beginning of our friendship, we were always high and drunk, he would see my kids for a few minutes and give them candy but not long.

I did not have any reason to bring him around them.

We were just friends and I never in a million years imagined that we would be here sober trying to get to know each other on a deeper level.

I had told him a few things about myself, and he had told me a few about himself but there was so much we did not know about each other.

This was the perfect time to get to know each other better.

We would lay in bed talking at night while the kids slept, asking each other questions when I realized I only knew him by his nickname.

I was lying in bed planning our future and I did not even know his first name.

So, he told me to guess if I wanted to know, and I did.

I guessed right on the first try. He thought someone told me and I thought he was lying but came to find out it was one lucky guess.

Things had changed quickly between us.

I could tell his feelings for me had grown overnight, so I asked him what had changed and that is when he told me the ultimatum I gave him!

It made him realize that I was the one for him.

A few days before we came to the hotel, we did not have any money and we were in my car feeling desperate when he asked me to go to the bar with him and flirt with some guys and to get them to come out back, where we would rob them and get a lick.

I looked at him like he had five heads and told him "I have three daughters and if you want to be around them and me you better check your way of thinking right now because about them, I don't play! AND DON'T!!

I would never do anything that can take me away from my daughters so don't ever ask me anything like that again!"

Then I told him God will provide he always has and always will, sure enough we figured it out well God did it.

He looked at me with the most surprised look and apologized to me telling me how much he respected me.

I realized how much I cared about him because immediately I wanted to protect him, to help him change his life and get him out the streets.

I knew that if I did not help him, he too would end up dead or in jail.

I made it my business to help him and not to focus on what was going on inside of me and without me even knowing I was suppressing all my feelings.

Things were difficult, social services were moving me from hotel to hotel so there was no stability for us.

Some hotels were decent, but we had some we could not even stay at.

I would have to get the room so they would continue to help me, but I would stay wherever I could for them nights until they found me a decent room.

I had to find work quickly, I had to get a place!

This was no life for my beautiful babies.

I started praying! I started asking God to lead me to help me find a place so that I can try to get my life together.

I had all my furniture in my cousin's garage, and I just wanted to be at home. It had been so long since I turned the keys to my own house since my children laid in their own beds, I begged God to please fix it for me.

I started looking for work and quickly I got a job interview where I would see God's hand. The interview was for a call center position but when I arrived it was like the angels were at the front door waiting for me! The owner decided he did not want to give me the position on the phones doing marketing, he wanted me to become his assistant and to my office I went.

I went from a cubicle and a phone to a full office where I would be running all his hundreds of rental properties!

I was in awe!!!

How did this happen???

It was only God who could open a door for me, in a place where there were no doors! I was working just a few days when the owner and I got to talking and he happened to ask me where I lived and what my situation was.

I explained to him that social services were willing to pay for a place for me, but that I was living in a hotel. I didn't find anyone who would take the vouchers. That man looked at me and said get your purse let's go! I was so confused but I followed.

He drove me to one of his rental properties, a two-bedroom house, in need of some minor repairs but in my eyes, she was beautiful!

I figured he wanted me to get our guys out to do the work, since that was part of my job and instead, he asked me will this work for you?

I was shocked and asked him to repeat himself. He repeated it again "will this work for you and your family?" With tears running down my face I just said "yes!"

He took the vouchers, fixed the house, and within a week God had turned my situation completely around. I was turning the keys to our new house!

The smiles on my kids face still fills my heart today as I write this.

There is no better feeling than to bathe your babies and tuck them into bed at night, how I appreciated that first night in our new house on 27 Hewitt St.

We quickly went to my cousin's house to get all my furniture. The furniture I had loaded into the U-Haul two months before.

I was so excited to see my things and to show my guy what I was like as a woman in the home. Things were going so well with us; I was looking forward to starting a new life and working on forgetting what I could of the past.

Funny how things do not work that way, it is crazy how a person can pretend everything is okay until they get into a place where they feel safe, and it all hits you like a ton of bricks and that is what happened to me. The furniture was in place, the house was clean, and the candles were burning.

We were sitting on the porch talking, kids were in bed, and he just looked at me and said, "wow I didn't know or imagine you were like this."

I said "What do you mean?"

He went on to explain that seeing me from house to house, sleeping in my car, and living in shabby hotels. He couldn't imagine who I was. I went from having all our clothes in garbage bags to having all our stuff together.

I had beautiful furniture and once I got my stuff in the house, I went to work and he saw my OCD go into play quickly.

I am over the top organized, I need every corner of my house to be cleaned, including drawers, closets and all that.

He never saw anything like it.

It was hard to see the real me after all the rumors he heard about me, because every day I gave him another reason to fall in love with me.

He respected my hustle, my determination, and that no matter what I went through I never looked like it.

He was digging me, I was giving him the love and the family he so desperately needed.

Everything was going well, until we made a big mistake. We put his late brother's picture in our bedroom. It was something we both agreed on at first.

He wanted to light a candle and we both loved him very much and respected him and had no reason not to want him with us. We both lost him!

We wanted to keep his memory alive. It was done with so much love and at first it was good for us. We would sit and share our memories. Laugh about him, we would cry together, and we were there for each other no secrets no lie just pure honest friendship that was growing into love.

Love comes extremely fast when you are sharing your life with someone who you are so deeply connected to. That too came with a new emotion, jealousy. I was starting to show signs of depression again. I was not getting out of bed, showering was a chore, curtains were shut, and I was no longer functioning.

The nightmares of watching him murdered, the guilt of not being able to save his life, and the feeling of total desperation when you know you will no longer see the person you expected to be with forever.

I was not over him; I was not over his death, his murder, or the fact that his daughter did not have a father and if he were not out with me then he would be here.

Guilt was killing me, and jealousy was brewing in my guy.

I cannot blame him for the way those feelings took over him back then because I cannot imagine how it felt watching me lie there in the dark when I was always upbeat and hyper.

At first, he was there for me, he laid with me and cried with me many times but then the panic attacks and the anxiety hit hard.

He would put me in the shower where I would scream, cry, and shake and he would stand in that shower with me holding me amid my storms. I had never seen such compassion in my life, I had never felt that way before, I knew depression and I knew sadness, but this was on another level and my guy held me down.

But I could not shake it off, I wanted to get up, I wanted to show him I was there and that I wanted to be with him!

I did, but the grief and the guilt beat me day after day.

My guy was getting worn out, I could feel the distance starting. I could see that I was pushing him away, but as much as I wanted to fight for us I could not.

Time had passed and his family and I had hatched things out.

With everything going on, from hotel to hotel, his mother got wind of my situation and opened her doors to my girls and I for a few days.

Of course, like a scene out of a movie, his brother came home from prison. You really cannot make any of it up. If I could put an emoji in this book, right now I would have them.

He went and told his mother about us, and she talked to my guy about it but he proudly said "I already know, she told me that in the beginning."

His mother lovingly pulled me aside and told me that she was no one to judge me.

For who can say they do not have a past and she took me as a daughter that day and I would always have a mother with her. So, everyone got over it.

She came to the house to visit, since I had not been by the house and that was not like us, we would come by every day.

Even if it were just to say hi from the car.

That is when she found me in the condition, I was in.

His Mother, but I prefer to say my mother if you do not mind, grabbed me, picked me up and sat me on her lap in my living room sofa and held me like a baby!

Then she said "Cry!" "Cry!" "Cry!" and "Let it all out!"

I cried my heart out and when I was done, she said "Now do you love my son?"

I quickly said "Of course."

She asked, "Do you want to be with him?"

I responded "Yes"

She said "Okay then that's it, let it go, forgive yourself, I don't blame you I want you to be free from this and be happy with my son! We are a family and we got you but if you don't go take a shower and look pretty and get back to who you are then you're going to lose him and I don't want that because I can sleep now that my son is here with you, I don't worry that I am going to bury another son so I need you to shake this off and fight! You can do it, I go for you, I believe in you."

That day it was a wrap, I took a shower got dressed and got back on, I was ready.

I got a job and started living life again, I was not going to lose my guy.

I was going to work, and I started noticing his change, his attitude was different, I was okay now but unfortunately now he was not.

I put doubt inside of his mind, he was questioning my love for him.

He was asking himself if I loved his late brother more than I loved him and those feelings would change him and make him into a person I was not ready to meet.

When I went back to work and started getting "cute" again, I expected to make him happy and glad to have me back in the game.

Instead, it made him jealous and made him question me and my loyalty.

The accusations started and my every minute was being calculated, I had to explain why I was late, and it was not something that I didn't want to deal with.

I was not going to go back to the toxic behaviors of my past.

Never say never!

Things escalated quickly one night, we were arguing and out of nowhere, he just slammed me into the dining room wall. It took me by surprise.

He apologized so quickly, and I knew he meant it.

I could see he was surprised by his own behavior. He had never done that before. I forgave him.

It wasn't long when we were in another heated discussion and this time he slammed me into the sofa.

It was so forceful, my head slammed into the wall and I literally saw stars.

I blacked out a little and I remember telling him, "when I get myself together you better not be here!"

He just stood there saying "sorry! Sorry! Sorry!"

I came to and he was there. I had warned him and given him time, but that was it if this guy thought he was going to touch me well then, game on.

I stood up and punched him so hard in his nose, blood gushed.

He chilled out for a nice while and things were okay but different, the innocence of our relationship was gone.

My cousins lived around the corner and that was perfect for me because they were the closest people to me, they were not my blood cousins, but we consider ourselves more than blood.

Those drinking days from our childhood, those fighting days, one of the epic memories was after beating this guy up, we threw potato salad on him! It landed on his jerry curls and we laugh till this day about it.

We were so bad, we would get their sister high, my big cousin, my favorite, and she thought she would see power rangers and we would play along just for kicks the good old days when prank calling was our game, and we were the masters.

We were terrible. We were going to be rappers one day. We even had our own rap group, and it was the best times during my worst times.

Living so close was amazing. They would come over and we would spend time together and my guy was cool, he did not mind, but he was acting strange, he was very isolated.

My cousins and I went by vibes, and we knew his energy was off and they were seeing red flags and I was ignoring them.

One day when they came over things got bad, my guy and I were outside arguing and he got into my car.

He did not have a license so I tried to get the keys from him, and I jumped in the window trying to grab them when he put that car in reverse and just took off with me hanging out the window.

My kids were screaming "Mommy!" my cousins were holding them, and I was holding on for dear life. It was so scary! I was not going out like that in front of my kids!

As soon as he stopped, I hurried off and walked home upset! He sped off in my car and there was nothing I could do but cry as my cousins lectured me about leaving. I do not know why but, I did not listen, I did not leave. I stayed, I loved him.

 I even jumped into a fist fight he was having in the middle of the busy South Broad St and Cass St. Intersection. I ran up from behind and hit the guy so hard, he fell out. I started stomping him out in my stilettos, about him I was ready.

But my loyalty to him was never clear to him, no matter what he would never trust me.Things continued to get out of hand, my dad and brother had to come over because of our fights.

I realized at that moment that I was putting everyone I love in the middle of this toxic relationship, but I did not want to leave. I wanted to be with him.

I knew that if we had any chances of making it, we would need to get God in the middle of this mess. I started talking to him about God. That did not go well, but he did not get in the way of me trying to go back to the Kingdom Hall but leave him out of it. So, I did. I started going back to the meetings trying to look for God.

It was good but then quickly the guilt, fornication, adultery, is all I was hearing.

I could not sit there comfortably when I knew I was married and living with another man. I needed to fix my life and I had to start making better decisions. I did not want this for my kids.

I wanted them to live a good life, one they could be proud of.

Then boom tragedy hit me again, I got the call that my Godmother passed away and that was a big loss for me. I still have her picture in my kitchen as if she is there counseling me and reminding me of the love that God has for me.

She left a message for her loved ones that was read at her viewing. She had them read James 4:8 "Draw close to God, and he will draw close to you." a scripture that I keep dear to my heart and has gotten me through life.I was devastated. How can the woman that practically raised me who I called "Mami" be gone.

How could this happen now when things are already hard. It just went with the schedule of my life one thing after another. This was another. I had lost a friend to gun violence also, so I was not in a good place, I do not think anyone was.

Chapter 10

Two years passed and I was still trying to live right and get my relationship with God right, so we decided we were going to get married but I had to get divorced first so I did.

I was getting a divorce and planning a wedding at the same time. I was driving cabs and saving money to have this dream wedding I wanted, but money was still limited.

I was the main provider. Although my guy would go with me to drive cabs, he did not have a job of his own.

My family was closer than ever! I was at my dad's house all the time; my father's wife and I were finally in a great place. She was there for me, she even bought me my wedding dress.

I couldn't be happier, I was planning this big wedding and finally all my dreams were about to come true, I mean I thought.

My guy had shown me a few red flags.Once we were all at my dad's house for rehearsals and some change went missing.My father's wife collected quarters and a noticeable amount was missing.

Quickly I questioned him because he was the only new person in our circle, everyone who was around had always been around and I knew he had a past that included stealing.

So, I was upset, but I forgave him, I was not going to not get married because of quarters I thought. We all moved on and we continued to plan the wedding.

A few days before the wedding we got into a bad fight because I couldn't let the quarters go. It was too much for me.

My mother had to call my father because we were throwing stuff and it got bad, my dad came, and he grabbed my guy by the face.

It got so hostile! I was so scared, I just broke everyone up and my father's wife was scared it was too much!Of course not enough to cancel our wedding. I was going to get married.

My father's wife even went all out for me and had a bridal shower for me. We had a blast. It was such a good time.

I wanted this feeling forever.

All of us together smiling, good food, that is something our family always did get togethers.

We were so weird one day we were killing each other the next thing we were having turkey for thanksgiving. It was toxic.

But when the good times came rolling in, I don't think anyone could deny the tough times were worth it. I loved them and no matter what I was grateful for all they were doing for us.

My father and his wife paid for a substantial portion of our wedding and went beyond to make this day special for me.

The big day was finally here, and it was beautiful everything was perfect, we had ice sculptures, fruit sculptures, floating candles, and rose pedals everywhere, it was bomb.

Our families were there to support us, and everything was perfect until he did it again, this time my aunt saw him take money out of my father's wife's purse.

What was supposed to be the best night of my life, turned out to be a big fight! Once again, he embarrassed me and broke my trust and heart.That would not be the worst of it. The news was just starting to come in. I was not ready.

Not even two weeks married, and it was as if he lost his mind.

I am sure the guilt would not let him come around me or what it was, but he went back to the streets, and I could not get him to come home.

I was heartbroken, I could not believe he was doing all these things to me.

Where was the guy who sat in the car with me when I was homeless? Where did he go? I did not know this person.

Soon I would be even more broken when someone close to me broke the news that the night of my bachelorette party my guy confessed, that he was getting sexual favors in a car.

I lost it, I found myself laying on the floor face down screaming, crying like I was the day my grandmother died when I was nine years old.

I had never felt this pain from a man, he broke me. I lost it that day. I got garbage bags and packed all his clothes up and I threw everything in the car and drove on the block where everyone was outside!

It's the hood.I started throwing all his clothes out of my car in the middle of the street right on the block. Everyone was stunned! Everyone called me crazy for all the fights, but now they really thought I was crazy!

They were not ready, that was just the beginning.

I was out there yelling his name, I knew he was there, he was hiding, and he was. I left all his stuff in the middle of the street and went home to cry like a baby.

I felt like I was going to die. The only person who had been there for me in my worst had become a monster that I did not know and did not want to know.

We were just married, and I wanted to live right with him. Finally, my family was together in a way that I could only dream of. This could not be happening. It was.

In the middle of all this, I lost one of my childhood best friends to Lupus. This was the second time I lost someone I love to this horrible disease.

My cousin who was more like my sister also lost her battle. Watching her lose her life,and now having to help clean out my best friend's closets and look at her four-year-old baby who would never see his mother again. It all seemed like too much!

Now this man who I just married had destroyed me. That did something to me, it changed me. I was out for revenge, I was coming for his throat. I was going to hurt him, and I was not going to be kind about it at all.

Enough was enough. The opportunity did not take long to appear. I paid him back the best way I knew how, I cheated too. Soon as I did it, I realized the only person I hurt was myself.

We had just got married and already we both had violated our marriage. My second marriage and it was already a mess. All I ever wanted since I was a child was to marry one person and have sex with only one person and live happy.

I was completely distraught. We already had a violent past; his mouth was beyond disrespectful, and my hands were too. One day he said the wrong thing and all I remember was hitting him with a belt buckle in his private part and he threw up.

It was bad but still we got married and now we are here. How did this happen? We went from Bonnie and Clyde to the police and the local drug dealers?

We were at war, if I saw him on the streets, he would call me every name under the sun except for two, the child of Christ and my own.

I would go as far as to try to run him over with my car more than once, it was toxic. Things quickly worsened, as if they could be any worse but there was.

He was so deep in the streets he joined a local gang and I had to give up our place due to a rat infestation that left my mother, my kids, and me homeless again. He had abandoned the home for the gang and the streets.

I was shocked but I had to make a move so I went to stay with my sister on Beatty St, where things would really get crazy.

I was down for a few days, having to leave my house. Mom was being knaggy complaining about everything. Kids were big now, so they were super lit.

The girls were riding bikes, playing in make-up, listening to music, singing, and dancing in the living room, they always filled my heart.

I loved watching them be kids, reminding me of all I missed.

My nephew was a teenager trying to get into trouble and being a boy in Trenton the streets called you and they were calling him. Titi is Spanish for Auntie, that is what they call me, and I was not having it.

I was out there hunting him down, at his school, the trap, wherever he was I was. I went as far as screaming his name all crazy in the street until the Old G's threw him out because I was making the spot hot. I ain't care that's my nephew! I thought.

All that meant to me was he is my son! The streets had taken too much from me, they were not taking him too. I went to war for him, and it paid off.

The one thing about my nephew was he never fought me back, never disrespected me, never questioned me, he would get in the car and go. I would beat his head in about all I was through explaining that I understood the streets and I understood him.

But the reality was the streets can only give you one of two things: prison or death. I was not losing him, and he knew I was not going to give up.

While I was fighting for my nephew and trying to keep him in the house, I was going through my own war with my husband and chasing him was part of my daily routine.

I would spin the block over and over again, looking for him and wanting him to see me, because I made sure I stayed beautiful outside because I refused anyone to see how ugly I was feeling inside.

I was at such a low point in my life, I had not gotten a break in two years since I left Texas. I was crying day in and day out wishing he would look for me, come find us but he was deep in, and he forgot about us. I was devastated.

I was smoking weed to make it through the day and my mother could not take that, so she left. She ran from me again when I needed her the most.

I know I was hard to deal with, I know I smoked weed and was not the picture she had of me, but I was messed up! I had so much pain going on, and all I needed was a believer and a supporter. Someone to guide me with love. Just be there.

I did not want my kids to ever smoke weed, and I did not do it in front of them, but I knew if they ever did that, I would not treat them anyway because of it. I was broken. My mother got on a plane and moved to Puerto Rico.

I was at my sister's house just sitting on the porch, trying to help her the best I could but I could barely help myself.

In the last two years I went through domestic violence, divorce, marriage, the murder of my first love, depression, PTSD, anxiety attacks and homelessness to say the least.

I didn't even know how I was still standing or where I was getting the strength to get through, then I looked at my girls.

Even though I knew I was not the mother they knew and that I was lost. I was there, I would never leave them or abandon them.

No matter where we went or how we got there if we were together, we had it all. I was grateful to have my sister's support and she was going through her own struggles and her own tough times but still she opened her home to me and I was wild.

I was a wild girl and had a lot to deal with, so I know that I was difficult. I started getting to know a few of the girls in the neighborhood and that was exactly what I needed. I needed to stop looking for my husband. I had to be stopped.

Enough was enough I had to find myself and love myself.

I was not perfect, but I was a very good wife. I cleaned, cooked, laundry, provided financially, and did not lack in the bedroom so why was I out here looking like a fool for this man. So, I stopped chasing him.

I became really close with the neighbor across the street, there was an instant attraction between us. At first I thought it was nothing serious, just physically.

She was in love with the father of her kids, and I was in love with my husband, but we were attracted to each other. We had so much fun together and it grew into a friendship immediately.

We knew that we both were exceedingly rare, pure hearted people that were both suffering.We were two women in love with men. Men who could not appreciate how amazing we were! We gave each other the support we needed, to get through those times without getting involved with other men.

I knew I did not want to feel that disgusting feeling I got again. The more time she and I spent with each other, the more we realized that there was definitely more between her and I. We immediately knew if we took it any further, we would be more than we were willing to give. We pumped our breaks really quickly. I scared her, just as much as she scared me.

That's a feeling that would never change, no matter how much time passes. She will forever be the what if?

My sister's sister-in-law came by to visit and we clicked.

It was like two peas in a pod. Immediate best friends, we had the same cars, same colors, sunroof, and we were ready to take over the town.

The fun started, no more crying over my husband, no more sitting on my sister's porch. Me and my new bestie were out.

We could not stop, we were having a blast with our kids and my sister's kids. Pack up the cars and go. I started hanging over her house more, no one knew where it was, and it was quiet.

My husband started noticing that I was not chasing him, so he came around trying to catch me doing something wrong. I was not, I was sitting on my neighbor's porch, and she had her two friends over.I was just sitting there smoking innocently and he lost it.

Next thing you know I was on the ground, and he had a knife to me. Someone called the police and they pulled up while he was on me and arrested him.

I had to be seen by the ambulance, I had a really bad panic attack. After that event, plus the fact that I was not able to work with everything going on. I was not able to help financially, I had to leave my sister's house.

I went to social service and told them that once again I was homeless, and I needed help. They told me that there was only one place they could send me and that was a homeless shelter for domestic violence victims.

I qualified to go to this special shelter because of my history of domestic violence. So, I had no choice but to go, so my kids and I got on the road to the place they sent us which was about thirty minutes away from Trenton.

I had to go to the local police station since it was a domestic violence shelter. You could not just show up, you had to be escorted by police.

As I was driving on the highway in the dark, I looked back through my rear-view mirror and just looked at my babies sitting in the back seat on another adventure. I was my mother all over again, now I knew how she felt all those times with us in the back. All those times we ran away from our problems.

Except, I was not running away, I was in Trenton, NJ where ALL my family lives and I was homeless.

As I drove, I figured I should call my husband and he would tell me to come to his mother's house and we could fix all this.

I just wanted to be safe in his arms again, so I put all my pride away and I called him. He answered, there were girls in the background, and he showed out. He was so disrespectful to me as I cried telling him I was on my way to a shelter with the girls.

I did not know what to do. He just savagely blew me off and told me it was not his problem, while the girls in the back just laughed and hung up on me.

My stomach sank, I was in utter disbelief but also in a pain that I could not bear for my children to see.

I called Louisiana to see if their father could help. He could wire me money for a room for the night, he answered and told me there was nothing he could do to help me. So now I arrive at the police station, desperate, nervous, anxious not knowing where I would be staying with my girls.

I imagined every movie shelter I could think of, and the thoughts just continued to run through my mind as I sat in the police station waiting for an officer to escort my girls and me.

I just looked at my babies as the two oldest cuddled up next to me and my youngest on my lap. How did I allow us to get here? I just smiled at them with tears in my eyes and assured them that we were going to be okay and that no matter what we were together.

I would never leave them ever. It was always us. I had failed them big time. At that moment I could only do what I did best when I was in trouble, so I began to pray.

Begging my God to please take us to a safe, clean place. To please send the angels to protect us and keep us covered because I was terrified. We followed the officer who drove us around the corner to the shelter and as we arrived it was as if God himself was waiting to receive us, it was a mansion.

A beautiful home turned into a shelter, only God could do a miracle like this. I am from Trenton. We do not have this; they do not send us to places like this! We get sent to hotels and if we are lucky, it is decent.

This was only God!

This place was immaculate inside, offices for us to talk with social workers who were there to help us get our lives together. They told me if I completed the program, they would move me anywhere in the area, and get me through school. I was excited for a minute, I could do this, I could get my life together I thought.

They enrolled my girls into the local school and got us in a room with three sets of bunk beds and explained that we could have roommates at any time, only one set of beds was ours.

I was not tripping since it was nice, and it had a playroom, nice kitchen, food, and a yard with a bench where I would sit and think looking at the biggest oak tree, thanking God for bringing me somewhere safe.

My mental health was so deteriorated. I was so hurt how could I be in a shelter with my daughters when I had a city full of family so close.

How could my husband do me that way, and the girls when he had been there for the last two years helping me raise them and they called him Daddy?

How could their biological father who had not seen them in two years and wasn't even on child support not willing to at least get us a room for a night or two?I wanted to dig a hole and crawl in, I was stuck.

I felt so lonely, for the first time I had no one, just my daughters and I as we laid on the bunk beds all four of us together. I watched them sleep as I laid there crying feeling like a complete failure.

I went to my bestie's house to try to get away with everything going on and I had to be back before curfew. I was waiting behind a taxicab that was blocking me from parking, when suddenly a girl came out of this house.

I forgot everything and everybody and I only had one mission and that was to find out who she was.

I ran in the house and told my best friend I had to meet her, and I was on the hunt. The next day she was on her motorcycle when I pulled up and almost hit her!

I was so excited. I never wanted to meet a girl like that before, I had attractions, but this was different, I wanted more with her.

I quickly apologized for almost killing her and she forgave me, it was history after that we were spending time together all day before I had to get back and she had a curfew too, so it worked out.

I stayed at the shelter for about a week, and I decided to visit my niece who lived on Washington St. It had been a while since I saw her with everything going on. I pulled up to her house and quickly she asked me where I was? I am one to always come around. I told her where I was staying, and she lost it.

My niece immediately said, "Titi you better go to that shelter right now and go get all your things and come here and I mean right now."

I said no at first because I knew that if I left the shelter, I was walking away from all the help they were offering me, and the chance to get in my own place. On the other hand, I would have to be there a long time and I was not in the right state of mind.

So, I took my niece up on her offer and came to stay with her leaving all those amazing opportunities behind.Now that I did not have a curfew and more time to spend with the girl, I was thinking about coming out for the first time in my life.

Liking girls was a big secret I had since I was a little girl. I liked girls before I liked boys, I am imagining that stems from the sexual abuse from childhood. Whatever it was I was finally coming to terms that these feelings I had were real and that I had to face them.

We were spending so much time together and although she had a lot going on and her own demons, I was good for her and vice versa. I was focused on something other than my husband for the first time in a long time, although I cannot lie, he was in the back of my mind.

I was not going to allow that to get in the way of this newfound feeling I was having. The girl and I were both catching feelings and the more time we spent together the more I knew that I had found more than anything a lifetime friend.

She was such a good person but like me, full of demons. We were both just masking our pain by keeping each other busy. At the time it seemed like a promising idea, but I was moving too fast, and I was not thinking about how my actions would affect yet another person.

I had her around my daughters, we were doing things together with them and I was really catching feelings for her.You cannot love anyone if you do not love yourself.

I did not feel worthy of love, how could I? I had been through so much and here I was jumping from one person to another without thinking about consequences.

We were driving around with my youngest daughter in the car when I saw my husband and all his friends standing on the corner. As I waited for the light to turn, he was mocking me.

Me being who I was, I had my four-year-old daughter flick him off.

In return, it made him pissed beyond words, he raised her and that was his baby, so the disrespect cut him deep.

He had to pay me back, but I was gone, so he went around my father's house and cursed his wife out from A to Z, then mooned her. They called me to tell me what was going on and one thing about me, I never was the one to play about my family and I was not playing about them that day.

I dropped the girl off and told her I would be back and drove around my father's house to confront him and that is exactly what I did. I picked my niece up on the way and I went looking, I found him and his "brothers" , what they called themselves, around the corner at Third St Park and I was mad.

 I was so angry that I immediately tried to pin him against a garage with my car and I did but he was getting out. I jumped out of the car, jumped on top of the car, and jumped like Wonder woman and punched him in the face.

They already knew that I was not right, that I was known for jumping out on him so they started running in the park mocking me, laughing because they knew I could not drive in the park, oops they thought.

 I drove that car in that park at full speed and all you saw was guys jumping out of the way and my husband running with all his might. I was trying to run him over. He landed on the bridge of the monkey bars and my car landed under it.

 I forgot my four-year-old was in the back. I forgot about my niece. I did not care; I was tired of the hurt I was feeling!

No one had ever hurt me the way my husband had, and he was about to understand. His cousin ran to my car begging me to please go, he kept telling me the police were coming and that I had to go.

He helped me push my car out because it was stuck and thankfully, he got me out of there. My husband was so scared, he never saw me go that far and that day he knew the extent of my pain, he felt it.

I was holding so many feelings inside, but this last time blew the top off my head.I was thinking of how he was laughing at me. He also had other people laughing at me when I was driving to a shelter with my babies, when I needed him the most.

He turned his back on me, all I saw was red and I was not done. I dropped off my niece that I had with me and went back to my other niece's house where I was staying to drop off my daughter because I was going to finish what I started.

I took about three shots to give me liquid courage, not that I needed it and got in my car and drove back to the hood to do damage.

I got back to Centre St and I quickly saw my husband and his crew. I jumped out trying to fight my husband, and quickly the attention was turned elsewhere when one of his homeboys tried to fight me.

That is when things changed quickly as they always did, my husband jumped in front of me and told him if he even dares to even look at me again that he would take him up and through there.

I saw my guy at that moment, the guy who stayed in the car with me when I was homeless, the one who was helping me raise my kids, the one who cared for me at my rock bottom, he was back. I just stood in shock, I had waited for so long for him to be on my side and now he was.

He grabbed me and said, "Look at you ma you're so drunk and you're willing out, please go get in the car and go, these people are dangerous, and you can get hurt please go."

I did not care and to be honest I was not scared of any of them. To me the only one who put fear in my heart was God, I was not going anywhere until he talked to me.

So, he promised if I went home that he would call me and we would talk, so I left.

A few hours later he came to see me, and we sat in the car and talked for hours just like old times, he cried, I cried. We were both broken, he was more lost than I thought.

I thought that he was living his best life, but he was just throwing his life away with bad associations, drugs, and alcohol to try to get over us. I was doing the same except now I had this girl involved and I had true feelings for her,

I told him, and I explained to him that I liked her a lot and had feelings for her but that we were legally married, and I was willing to try to fix our marriage if he was willing to leave the streets.

Even though I had these deep feelings for this amazing girl, I wanted to save his life. I had an obligation to his brother, and I did not want to lose someone else. Never thinking of myself, or the girl that was stealing my heart.

Immediately he looked crazy like I said something insane, but I did not know the only way he could leave the streets was with his life.

I had no idea how deep he was in. I broke up with the girl, and she was completely devastated. I hurt her so bad, and I did not even know the extent of it. I had no idea that my actions would cause such a domino effect on her life.

Things changed overnight, I look back and I know all she went through for the decision I made to go back to my husband.How it destroyed her life but when I think of what happened next, I never regret leaving her that day. I know I saved both of our lives.

A girl was murdered in front of her daughters because of her relationship with the same circle my husband was surrounding himself with. The same guys I tried to run over a few days earlier. Things got crazy in the city and fast.

I did not know anything about it.

My husband and I were at my niece's house talking, and I know today that if all that had not happened to get us back together that he would be in prison today.

When he found out all that happened and someone innocent lost her life, and the thought of her daughters was too much for even him to bear.

He realized that all this time, I had been fighting for his life, for his future! I wanted his best the whole time, all I wanted was to be happy with him and it all became clear. I was so worried about his life I forgot about mine.

I forgot about my feelings towards this woman who had forever changed my life. I now was back to my lie; I mean life as a wife.

Trying to save someone's life while depriving myself of one. So, I gave him an ultimatum to drop the streets or drop me. But he could not have both. Since I could not have my one.

It was Halloween night when I was outside with the kids and out of nowhere my husband showed up looking like a ghost, he tried to leave the gang, and he ended up running from gunfire and almost lost his life.

He was standing in front of me telling me we were going to die next, that they were coming for us too.

I tried to save his life, but now the lives of my daughters and I were in danger.

Thankfully, no one knew where I was staying at the time, and I just grabbed my babies, and we went upstairs to talk. What were we going to do?

We had no money, no place to go, and there were people looking for us to kill us. I could only do one thing, you know it, get on my knees, and pray.

I went to God, he was in control, and I could not forget now. The bible clearly states, "not to lean on your own understanding" and this was not the time to try to figure things out myself.

I cried out to God that night as my husband and kids slept, we were sleeping on the same floor I slept with my girl on, and I could not help but to be thinking about her too.

I was confused, here I was in a situation where I could lose my life and my kids' life for a person who left me in a shelter.

While I was sure I had someone crying and hurting because of me.

I was hurting too, I missed her so much, I knew what we had was real. I just wanted to find her. I felt horrible, sick to my stomach, and all I wanted was God.

I cried and begged for him to heal her heart, to heal mine, but to save us to save my husband and my kids because our lives were in danger, and I needed to get out.

The very next day I was sitting on my niece's sofa looking like a zombie, as if I were waiting for something, and out of nowhere the phone rang.

It was social services, first I must say that was unheard of for welfare to call you, you had to wait all day to see someone, yet they were calling me.

They called to notify me that they owed me nine hundred dollars in cash and seven hundred in food stamps and that my money was already on my card. All I could do was cry, God did it again, he did, he really did it! Now it was time to act and that is exactly what I did!!!

Chapter 11

I quickly ran to the ATM and took out the cash and went to the grocery store. I loaded my trunk with nonperishable food, all the clothes I could fit, and a nineteen-inch tv for my babies.

I said goodbye to my niece, my husband and I went and said goodbye to his mom, and we got on ninety-five south crying like babies.

He was crying over his mom and me. Well, I was crying over her.

We had no destination and nowhere to go, the only thing we had was nine hundred dollars, what we had in our car, and each other.

Again, I would have to sacrifice myself in order to save many, it was really time to start putting full trust in God! It was clear dying was not his purpose for us and we didn't have a plan.

I figured as we started driving that the best place to go was Georgia because although I didn't have anyone there, I lived there before, and I knew my way around.

I also knew my mother had some Jehovah's Witness friends that still lived in the area and I figured that would be the best bet.

My husband had never left Trenton before, so he was having an extremely tough time. He was and is a complete momma's boy and leaving her was too much for him to bear.

My heart was hurting for him, but also for myself and at that point all I could think was drive this car as far as you can as quickly as you can and never look back.

After a sixteen-hour drive, we finally arrived in Georgia.

My husband was shocked to see how I could drive all of them hours by myself without stopping, but little did he know the road was my second home and driving was my therapy.

We arrived in Roswell, GA where I lived years before and we pulled into the first hotel we saw off the Holcomb Bridge Rd exit.

We paid the hotel for one week and that left us with enough money to eat and gas for a week, so the next day I went to a local temp agency and started working the next day.

Three days in Georgia and already I had a job in a professional environment feeling like somebody, but in the back of my mind all I could think about would anyone find us here and was this girl, okay? What had I done?

To save a life, I had to destroy another and my own. I was so hurt, and with no way of contacting her, life would have to go on.

We both acted as if we had no worries but by his nightmares, I knew we both were lying.

The week was almost up, we were basically homeless, and again I prayed. I called my mom who was still in Puerto Rico and told her my situation and she reached out to one of her Witness sisters.

I was disfellowshipped at the time, which means no one could talk to me, but this sister was no regular witness; she was a true follower of Christ.

God wanted me to see that he was there, and that I needed to get back to him, my way was not getting me anywhere.

The witness sister went out of her way and helped us get an apartment the same day we had to be out of the hotel. Only God!!

I will repeat this a few times, but I cannot help it, it is the truth!

God's best strategy is "SURPRISE" he always surprises me when I believe I saw his best, he shows me that I have not seen anything yet!

He came through again! He somehow was able to get us a two-bedroom two bath apartment in a beautiful, gated community with so many amenities including a pool.

How did this happen? As if he was telling us sleep okay you have security, and I am not talking about the gate!

He was our security, he would protect us, and he was not finished with us.I could not believe it. I got paid the same day and had enough money to pay the deposit and the rent and get us moved in.

How can you not pay attention to God? He will make you pay attention if you do not, and finally I was paying attention.We got the keys to our new apartment.

We moved in all our clothes, blankets, pillows, nonperishable foods, and our nineteen-inch T.V. that was all we had. We were grateful beyond words.

We had life and as I sat on the balcony of that empty apartment sitting on crates, I could only cry and thank God that he got us out! There was a young lady who was not so lucky, and her life mattered to me.

I could not forget the pain that I could only imagine her family were feeling, and as a mother of three young girls knowing that could have been me. It was my reality. It made me feel uneasy. We were laying down that night on our blankets in our room when the threatening calls started.

People telling us they were going to find us and kill us. Back then we had chirps and it kept going off all night.

My husband laid there feeling some type of way because his decisions influenced my daughters and me. I cannot imagine the heart it took for him to leave everything behind to give my girls and I a different life.

That is how silly my way of thinking was. He knew me, he knew I was never going to give up.

I would never let the streets win, I was willing to do anything to get him out the streets, I could not see another person I love die to our hood.

The reality is, I did not choose to be with a gang member. I had a chance more than once to choose that life, but I did not.

I was a leader not a follower, and I chose better back then.

He chose this after we were married, he chose this for us. Now I was here boosting him up, encouraging him for a decision that he made without thinking about us.

I was no better! I was not thinking about my kids or my life when I was out there going to war with these people, who did not have a problem murdering a mother in front of her kids. I was playing with fire, and he knew it.

I was so naïve, that I believed that instead of watching me lose my life he risked everything to save my life. The reality was, I had it backwards, I risked everything, even my kid's life, and my own to save his.

As I laid on that floor by his side, my heart raced listening to the threats coming through and we both just laid there eerily quiet, not saying a word.

All I could do was pray.

I kept working and for the first week we only had enough to eat white rice and water. We got lucky for a few days and had corn.

It still hurts my heart writing this thinking about my little girls, how grateful they were in that empty apartment playing together and how they never complained even when we only had rice and water.

I got my first check after moving in and I got us food, my daughters a full-size bed and I ran to goodwill and bought them out of every barbie they had.

I even got them a small Barbie house. I was so excited to bring it to them, they did not care that it was used, my baby girls were so happy.

They were good, I got them the cutest bed set with a canopy and they were beyond grateful. Things were finally coming together. I could see hope.

I was praying more than ever. I started going to the meetings again and began fixing my life to the standards of what I thought I had to reach to be right with God.

Studying the bible was a big part of my day which helped me immensely to start getting my life in order. I had been so far from God for so long and I had been living recklessly without care now I was in fear all the time.

I was constantly looking over my shoulder, worrying wherever I went. I had never felt so insecure before and God would constantly remind me that he was my security I had no reason to fear.

I continued to go to the meetings and my husband was also going since he felt indebted to the sister for helping us with our place. Plus, with our life in danger even he realized his need for God.

We enrolled the girls in school, but it was tough for me as a mother knowing my children did not even have a sofa to sit on, a table to eat and the holidays were approaching. My heart was hurting.

I remember I went to pick up my daughter from her class and her teacher pulled me aside and said, "Your daughter told me that you guys are having a tough time and told me a little bit of your situation and my parents, and I want to come by your house and bring some gifts."

I just cried. I bawled. She hugged me, how I needed that hug. I needed to feel the love of humanity.

I needed to see the love of Christ in person so that I would not give up, a moment when I was disheartened, a moment of weakness, when I was feeling lowly God once again moved his hand and touched this teacher to show kindness to my family.

They came and they brought so many gifts for my girls from barbies to holiday dresses we were beyond grateful and made me want to serve God more.

My mind was set that the best life was a life lived for God and he continued to bless me.

I was reinstated as one of Jehovah's Witnesses so now everyone could talk to me again. I now had the support of all the witnesses, from that two-bedroom apartment we went to a three-bedroom, two bath.

My nephew came to stay with us, my mother came back to live with us, the family had grown, and things could not be better.

My brother came to visit from Puerto Rico with my nephew and we drove to Texas for my sister's 25th wedding anniversary.

Our family was back together and for the first time in a long time there was nothing but love.

My other sister came down for the big event and for the first time since we were babies, I was in the room with four of my siblings at the same time.

I could not be more grateful to God for changing my life around. Especially, when in the back of my mind was the question, "Where is my baby brother?"

A question I still ask every day, especially with the years passing and still not a clue of where he may be.

What if this book will help more than I can imagine? What if somehow, he will find me. When you believe how I believe, I know better, I know I wrote that all wrong, let me rephrase especially for those in the back. "I will find my baby brother sooner than I can imagine in the mighty name of Jesus!" and I look forward to loving him for all the years I have missed out on.

Things continued to get better for us. My husband and I were both working and doing things in a way that pleased God, we had bible studies at our house, yes, our house.

God had even upgraded our home. We were in a three-story home with a mother-in-law suite for mom, fireplace, tree house in the yard, and a swing in the front of the house.

God showered us with his blessings. We were secure and we had everything we could ever want.

About four years had passed and things were great. I was spending time preaching, knocking door to door telling people about God's promise for the earth. How he wanted people to come to him and I even had a few bible studies.

I was teaching others about the bible, and I was loving it. I had amazing friends who were blessings in my life. I remember my sister's friend made me feel like a pretty woman!She took me to the mall and bought me the most elegant, classy outfit, then the four of us girls got dressed up, went to dinner in one of ATL" s best restaurants!

We watched the Phantom of the Opera at the FOX theater. I was living my best life. Box seats and driving in her brand-new Benz!God can truly take you from the pit to the palace I thought that night. I went from a shelter to Atlanta's hottest strip!

 I thought I was J-Lo walking through, you could not tell me anything as we walked through that romantic café for a glass of wine and a late dessert! Now this is how they are living on Love and Hip Hop and stuff!!!

 If you know me, I have a Tiffany Haddish personality, with some Cardi B, and some Queen Latifah, we can set it off , type of personality so yes, I was lit!! lit!!! And yes, I said it twice. I could get used to this.

My daughters were doing great, they were in wonderful schools and spiritually they were growing side by side with me. I was taking them out preaching and they loved it, they were always ready to serve God.

I was taking the time out to study the bible with them, to mentor them, and to be there like a mother should be. I remember playing outside with them on the swing, watching them play on their tree house from the top balcony, staring at the fireplace on chilly nights, it was amazing.

We were always busy doing things with our kids like taking drives through Georgia to find beautiful waterfalls and climbing to the top of Stone Mountain. Life was perfect. Which means, here comes trouble in paradise.

One day I was cleaning our bedroom closet when I ran into my husband's secret stash of pornography, and to all the men reading this you are thinking "So what?"

To that woman who found that stash it was a sign of betrayal.

My husband knew the way I felt about his personal addiction in the past, and me being the insecure woman I was, it was the same as cheating.

I had a horrible past and pornography was part of that past it made me feel bad about myself, it had nothing to do with him but at the time I could not register the information correctly.

I lost it, I went to our job where we both worked and I confronted him, he knew I was terribly upset. I left and went home but something inside me died right there and then. It was a major betrayal for me, but I did not handle it appropriately.

Instead of working things out and talking to him to figure out what was going on with us, with him. I just detached myself from him and the marriage. I made up my mind that I was done, I could not trust him anymore and I was not hearing any reason.

He came to me begging me to forgive him to give him a chance to get help because his addiction came from his childhood.He was praised for it even welcomed to it, for me it was something that took me to a bad place.

We both were trying to deal with our past, he was fighting an addiction, and I was still carrying all those stories I have written up to now. Instead, I was just compressing them the whole time.

I was still me inside of that nice house, that nice car, that decent job, and in that Kingdom Hall it was still me. I was still scared worrying about my past, and I was still walking around smiling when inside I was dying, still carrying around all the pain of years of hurt.

That one little thing made it all come bubbling up. I would not go near him, I locked myself in my daughter's room, all the things that we had been through were now running through my mind again.

I remember telling him since you do not want a good church woman, someone clean who gives all to God, I am going to be the woman you are watching on these tapes, the woman that makes you watch them instead of me. He started going to church without me, which fueled my fire even more instead of calming it.

I was begging him for so long to go to the meetings with me, but he stopped going long before this and he refused. I would try so hard to have him participate in things that would strengthen our marriage and draw us closer to God as a couple, but he had refused.

Now that I refused to go back to the kingdom hall, because of something he did to hurt me, he wanted to go just so he can get me back. I was so angry, and he even went as far to call the elders of the congregation to try to help us, and get me to fix our marriage, but I would not bend.

If I could go back in time that would be the moment that I would have bent and allowed them to help us, but I did not and the devil boy the devil, he always seizes the opportunity. There was a fellow co-worker of ours who so happen to be a lesbian and prior to the issue between my husband and I, we never talked. We did not converse about any of that, the minute this happened this girl started talking to me out of nowhere.

Next thing she and I were flirting, and it was clea. My husband could tell that we were flirting and that pissed him off. He went from bringing me food, going to the meetings again, and putting in the effort I had been asking for the whole time to packing his bags and without a word he went back to New Jersey.

When I checked the bank account, he had emptied it, and when I got home from work the lights were cut off. This man cut my power off and took all our money. I was pissed, I was bitter and angry before this and now he had really done it. I called him and we got into a bad argument where he wished death on my kids and myself.

Those words broke me, words to me hurt more than anything, I never did good with words. Maybe because I could never use words to hurt anyone the way they had been used to hurt me. I would do the next best thing to hurt someone who hurt me. I got involved with the girl, see in my eyes you left for a feeling, but now it is going to be an action.

I went back to sin full force, and I did not think about God, how it would affect my daughters, how leaving God would come with profound consequences, some that even I could not imagine or see coming.

I was dealing with the girl and my mother was heartbroken, I devastated her. We had everything; God had blessed us beyond words.

We could not think of a want we lacked nothing, but here I had become like the Israelites. I slapped God in the face, I went to the elders to confess my sin and they cried and begged me to stop what I was doing and to change there was no need to disfellowship me, we could fix it they said but I was gone.

I look back now, and it was like I was truly fighting another person inside of me. A person that has been there since I was a little girl. I could not think or see straight. As much as it hurt me to hurt them, I wanted to have the opportunity to figure out who I truly was.

I cried and told them I was sorry, but I was not going to change. The truth was I wanted to be free to be a lesbian and that was that.

I left and I remember driving to the local grocery store where I parked and just cried. I cried begging God to forgive me, asking myself what had I done? What had I done? I wanted to go back and tell them I changed my mind; I did not want to be disfellowshipped, I did not want to lose my spiritual family, but it was too late.

This time I was going to choose me. I was disfellowshipped soon after and I was not happy at all. I did all these things, and I was miserable.

Things didn't work out between the girl and I, because she had a girlfriend that she had recently broken up with. We both had baggage and could not love anyone or be there for anyone. I was lost and so was she.

 I was losing my mind; I tried dating others and that did not help me at all, just made me feel worse and worse about myself. I sat with my mother who was completely affected by what was going on with us and we decided to go on a road trip to Florida.

 My mother's best friend lived in Orlando, and it was a suitable time to do what we were good at running away when things were blurry. It was all part of God's plan.

We went down and we spent time with her best friend, and I reunited with her daughter who was one of my best friends growing up. I went with her to her house, and we had an amazing time.Her house for what I saw was beautiful. The next morning, I headed back to my mom, and we went back to Georgia.

On the ride back my husband called me, and we started to talk and make a mend. We decided that we should give it another run and that he wanted to come back home.Him in Trenton was scary for me because there were people who still wanted him dead.

We spoke about him coming back but he really did not want to live in our house just because of the way things had gone down before he left, we wanted to start over. This starting over is a thing I do that keeps me going, and never giving up!

I prayed about it and asked God to forgive us both and to lead us that although we had failed him that we wanted to fix things, not to let us go. A day or two later my friend called me from Orlando and told me she had to move to Ft Lauderdale, that she had a job offer and needed to rent her house out. Then she asked me, if I wanted to move, that she would rent me the house.

If that was not a sign from God, then I do not know what was! My husband came back to Georgia, and he brought my nephew with him to help us with the move to Florida. We rented a U-Haul, loaded it up, and off we were! Once again, we did what we did best… run! Or better yet, Start All Over!!!

Chapter 12

We arrived in Kissimmee excited to be in the sunshine state and ready to start a new life. So much had happened that we were ready to move forward and not look back.

We arrived at my friend's house, and I could tell right away her energy was off, but I figured it was overwhelming for all of us to be there. I brushed it off, even though if you know me, you know I am never wrong.

It was a lot of us, and we were planning to stay there for a few days until she left for Ft. Lauderdale, and then we would move in.

I thought of it as a vacation with my girl and I was looking forward to a big slumber party with my family and my besties family. Unfortunately, that was not how it went. Instead we found ourselves in a difficult situation. Nothing new, even you know that by now.

Immediately upon arrival my husband and nephew went and opened the garage to unload the U-Haul because we had to return it the next day, and that is when the nightmare began. First the garage was supposed to be empty so that I could put my things there until she left in a few days, that was the purpose of me coming a few days early.Also it was so she could show me around since I had never been to Florida except for that weekend.

The plan was that she would take me around town to show me where everything was and help me get set up with a job. I was excited about helping her out and renting her house so she could go on her new endeavor. It was a win, win situation until they opened that door.

The garage was full to the max, this garage had never been open by the spider webs I could tell. My husband and nephew looked at each other then looked at me, I looked at them in complete disbelief as my heart sank thinking what did we get ourselves into?

That was not the worst part, the worst part was when my nephew looked down and noticed a dog leg. Yes, just the leg, no body, no nothing just the leg. We were not even able to deal or react to the leg because immediately fleas started jumping everywhere and at that point, we picked up the leg and closed the door.

That night we slept in the living room and all night we were up because the fleas were biting us, they were everywhere. I talked to my friend, and she was obviously embarrassed and completely overwhelmed.

I was completely understanding and compassionate because she was going through a separation and was clearly going through a lot of things herself, so the least I could do was help. We called someone who came out and took care of the fleas and she moved to her new place, and we stayed behind as new renters. Everything was finally in its place. The last box was put away and after a dip in the pool we sat down in the living room to relax and watch a movie.

Just that quickly things changed again. There was a truck outside and my nephew came to let me know, it was someone named FPL. If you are from Florida, you already know where I am going with this. It was the light & water company my friend owed money and they were there to shut it off.

My husband and I begged and pleaded with him but there was nothing he could do. We were sitting in the dark with no water trying to figure out what to do next. I tried to call my friend and she told me that I was on my own and that there was nothing she could do. I sat there with tears in my eyes. I was filled with hurt and anger, but also realizing that I had it all and that I chose to leave God and lean on my own understanding.

I went from the palace back to the pit. I prayed to God to help us because we were in Florida where we did not know anybody. After praying like an angel, the neighbor came around and started talking to us. We told him everything that was going on and just like that he went to his house brought us a two-range propane camping burner to cook on.

Then he told us to use his hose and get all the water we needed. If it were not for God sending us that angel, I honestly do not know how we would have survived the next few days. I remembered that my niece lived in Orlando, and I reached out to her, she came immediately to my rescue.

We talked to her landlord and within twenty-four hours we were moved into a two-bedroom apartment and even though it was a tiny matchbox it was home. I could not have been more grateful to God.

I quickly found a job at a storage facility as an Assistant Manager and was able to provide for our family.

I excelled quickly and they saw so much potential in me, they promoted me within a month and transferred me to Stuart, FL. They gave me a paid three-bedroom apartment with two bathrooms. I had no expenses and a salary. I was the new Property Manager at a brand-new facility ten minutes from the beach.

God had shown me favor once again. I could see God's hands all over my life, I was working for an amazing man who cared about his employees, and I was beyond blessed. The pay was outstanding, and I was in love with my job.

I was meeting new people every day and networking for the storage facility everywhere I went. The storage was filling up rapidly, the owner was so impressed he gave me a raise after a raise plus commission.

I went from the three-bedroom apartment to a five-bedroom house with three bathrooms and a huge pool. It was so big I thought we had to share it, but it was ours.

I got my mother back and I was serving God again, my husband and I were still in the vicious cycle of so many break ups and make ups, even recently we had been going through our ups and downs again.

We were still hanging on or whatever you wanted to call it. The more I tried to get right and get our things in order the more fighting between us, we just could not get past the past.

No matter how many years had passed, He would not let me forget and I still had the same feeling inside of me, I liked women.

I maintained my friendships with a few women from my past, and although we were only friends, that deep connection was there, and it was real. I always hear the same thing, I do not know why you keep trying with this man, when we all know you like women.

"I look like a woman, but I think like a man."

Things were getting out of control between us, and communication was not something we knew how to do. Instead of talking and resolving problems we would scream, shout, and never did we think of how we were affecting my mother, nephew, and kids.

So many times, things got out of control, my husband used his mouth as a weapon, and I continued to use my hands and violence. I threw a pool ball at his head and thank God he ducked if not I may have been in prison today writing this.

The anger I felt from the name calling and the disrespect that would come from him was not something I would walk away from; he was going to feel how I felt. My performance at work was being affected by the problems at home and my owner was quickly noticing my light dimming out.

I could see I was losing everything: my home, my marriage, and my job. My mother was at her breaking point, and she booked another flight to Texas. I was so hurt that I told my husband to go too, and I was done. I got myself a small two-bedroom duplex for my daughters and I so we can move forward. I was done living in this toxic relationship that was destroying everything I love.

My husband was so hurt by my decision to give up our house and leave him that we got into one more heated fight, but this time he locked himself in my daughter's room after disrespecting me. I was broken and there was no stopping me, my nephew was begging me to stop but I was determined to get into that bedroom and put hands on him for his filthy mouth.

I had a bat in my hand, and I kept kicking the door in, my nephew continued to get in the middle to stop me and I remember telling him to get out of my way but his love for me would not allow him too. Instead of me walking away I hit my nephew with the bat over the head and I had never put hands on him in his life, I was broken but I broke him.

I was in a rage I could not see straight, I broke in the room and just jumped on my husband swinging on him, with no letting up. They finally both got out of there and my mother took them to the bus station where they got on a bus back home. My nephew was so heartbroken with me he did not even say goodbye, that is when my actions hit me.

That's my son I thought, how could I be so enraged that I would not stop myself even for my nephew who holds the key to my heart.

I lost my job immediately after, my mother left, and now it was just my girls and me once again. Depression came so fast I do not know what hit me. My kids were off to school, and I would get in bed until they got off the bus at two thirty. It went on for days.

Until one day my oldest daughter came home from school and looked at me with the saddest eyes and said "Mommy please come take a shower and get out of bed we need you!"

That hit me like a ton of bricks. With tears in my eyes, I quickly got up and got back to life, I forgot who was watching and I had to get up and fight.

I joined the gym, and I was busy with my girls, trying to figure things out and help them deal with their father leaving, because although he was not their biological father, he raised them and that was the only Daddy they knew.

 They were taking it hard and although they were not telling me how they felt they were acting out. Day in day out calls from school my two oldest daughters were fighting, even once they were about to fight each other in school. It was getting out of control.

I had to contact my husband, we talked and before you know it, he was on a bus back home. About his daughters he was not playing, and he knew they needed him, and he needed them too.

 I realized then that it was not only about us it was about them. Thinking back was this how things were? or was I still fooling myself?

I was happy when my husband came home or I was filling a void, one that I had tried endlessly to fill with no success. I was in a hole. I was not working. I had let everything fall apart and he was not home long before we had to move again.

This time we had no money and nowhere to go so I called my cousin in West Palm Beach and with no hesitation she told me to pack up and come stay with her, so we did.

Things at my cousins could not be better, we had family around and it was nice to spend so much time with my cousin since she has been such a big influencer in my life.

My cousin is the greatest woman I know, through all her struggles she has managed to still pick herself up and make it in a world that has done nothing but try to destroy her. I learn resilience from her and arduous work. My cousin to me is my hero and I am forever grateful to her.

My husband and I tried daily to find work so we could get a place of our own. Unfortunately, that never happened, and things were not going too well for my cousin either, she was selling her house and we all needed to figure out our next move.

With a heavy heart my husband and I realized that we had no more choices; we had to go back home to Jersey.We packed up again, filled another U-Haul and we got on the road to Trenton. After so many years of hiding and staying far from a place that haunted me in my dreams I was going back.

My husband and I prayed and asked God to watch over us. We did not know where we were going or what we were going to do, but we knew that God was leading the way as he always had.

Soon we arrived in Trenton and quickly my cousin let me stay with her for a few days until I could figure out what to do next. Then we went to stay with my sister-in-law, my husband's sister. Things were okay for a few days and then all hell broke loose, our kids got in a small argument over a brush that led to something that could have been avoided if we knew how to communicate as a family.

Unfortunately, in our culture and the way we were both raised it seemed talking was the only thing we did not do. I could see the result of how we were raised pouring out of us, and now our children.

We had to move out that day immediately and back to the homeless we were, I just sat in my car with my husband and kids crying like babies.

What were we going to do, how did we get back here?

I started making calls quickly to all the places for rent on craigslist and just like that I had an appointment to see an apartment and even faster we had the keys to our small apartment that we would call home for the next four years.

1418 Hamilton Ave, I could not believe how God did it again. I went from being homeless and in my own tiny home all in the same day only God can do something so big.

I was completely grateful. We moved in and for a little while everything was okay.

We had to watch our backs but that was normal in Trenton anyway, so we just did what we did all our lives, survived.

We thought things were okay until one day my husband was chased and shot at, thank God he ran and made it home.

I know the Angels were covering him.

He had been hit with a pistol and almost shot but the gun jammed recently on his last visit home, now they were trying to kill him again.

My husband was shutting down and he started getting really depressed.

I wanted to help him get his mind away from things, so after saving enough money I came up with the idea that we should have a baby. Since he raised my daughters but never had a child of his own.

Our kids were older now, our oldest was about sixteen so we knew time was ticking. I had my tubes tied in 1999 after my last daughter so we would have to get a tubal reversal to have a child.

We paid five stacks and we went to North Carolina so I could have the reversal done so that I could give my husband a child of his own. Everything went well. It was nice to just get away together without the kids, my mother had come down to watch them and help me recover from my surgery.

We took the train there and the train back. We had such a wonderful time on the trip and coming home we could not be happier thinking we would soon have our own baby that would change everything and finally we would be happy.

Boy did the universe have a completely different plan.

We were back and I had recovered so we were out spending time together with my brother when we ran into my husband's good friend. I had met him years back.He was the big homey who my husband's brother had introduced me to so proudly all those years back.

Ten years earlier when me and my husband had just got together, we ran into him and my husband introduced us again, and we clicked. We became so close that we even rode to downtown Trenton to get my husband some clothes for his birthday.

We were so close, and I always enjoyed our conversations since he was just like me, a deep thinker. He had gone to prison, and we lost touch except for once he sent his love to my brother who was doing time at the same prison.

Ten years passed and when we saw each other, it was a movie. It was so innocent, we were screaming and hugging it was nothing but love. My husband was so happy it was a big reunion.

We quickly made plans to hang out that weekend and I asked him, "big bro what's your favorite meal and I will cook it!" and I did. That weekend we picked him up and he came over for dinner just as planned. Everything was all love. We talked, hung out, and the three of us just laughed and reminisced.

Afterwards, I told my husband that we should give him a tour of our apartment. I was immensely proud of our modest home. We walked around the apartment and he quickly noticed my stack of books sitting on the table and he asked, "Who reads these books?" I quickly said it was me and he was taken back, he was a big reader also.

We went outside and my husband stood and let us both sit, and we were talking for what seemed like hours. I remember turning and looking at him when I noticed a scar on his face, and I touched it innocently and said oh my God, it is a butterfly. He had a scar on the side of his face in the shape of a butterfly, and everyone knows I love butterflies.

Butterflies have always been my thing.

This was a man who spent most of his life in prison, and now I had softened his face. He was a big man, but his personality was even bigger! I could see in his face how that touched him, but I did not try to read into it.

`We started talking and I felt so comfortable with him, and I trusted him with our marriage, so we began to talk about the things that my husband and I was going through, and he was listening to us both go back and forth like he was our marriage therapist, and we did not even think twice.

We were so naive, and immature. I was feeling so unappreciated at the time and my emotions were so high since my husband had changed so much since we had been back. I was fighting for his attention, his love, and most importantly I did not trust him.

Recently a girl from his job came knocking on our door with her man accusing my husband of trying to get in the bed with her. I sent her packing and told her she better never come to my house again. I was so ashamed, especially since my kids were there and saw the whole thing.

My husband was so far from the man I wanted in my life. He was back stealing and even embarrassed my daughters by stealing their coaches' phone at the last award ceremony. Looking back, I had no respect for him. I had losts it all, as we were there talking about our issues with his friend.

 Out of nowhere his friend just looked at me and said, "You know you're such an amazing woman and you're so strong" He could not get another word out; I was balling and crying. I reacted like I had never received a compliment before and that broke his heart but all the meanwhile my husband was untouched.

 His friend was a natural born leader, and everyone respected him, so he quickly got up and told my husband, "Hug your wife bro." He did, but the fact that someone had to tell him to hug me, turned me off. I did not want his hug anymore.

His friend tried to talk to him and give him advice, but my husband was far away from me and from reality. Seems like when things got dark for him, he pushed me clear out the way. I was so hurt, but I kept going.

 I was spending more time with his friend only because he was so easy to talk to, we would spend hours talking about some of the deepest things you can talk about in life. All the spiritual things that most people ignore daily. It was clear we were both gifted to see God in a way that I never saw before.

I felt like I lived my life trying to explain to people how real God was and how I had seen his hand so many times, but for the first time someone got me. I could not wait to talk again, it became addictive. I got dropped off out south Trenton just to come hang out with him and his sister and it was a fun time every time.

I was not feeling good, so I figured I should take a pregnancy test since, we were trying, it was positive. I was finally pregnant, after ten years we were going to have a child of our own, so I got up and ran to my husband's job to tell him he was happy.

I went down to his friend's house to give him the news and to talk some more, because it was like his brain was calling mine. I told him, let us go to the park. I wanted to take a walk, so we did.I noticed that he was acting so weird, he never looked uncomfortable before when we talked but this time, he was not himself.

I told him we should leave so we did, we walked and talked but the whole time I could feel his energy was completely off, what was going on? We kept walking and we got back to his house, and something was still off, I could not put my finger on it. Then his sister said, "I see the way you both stare at each other, that's not good!"

We laughed and told her we did not know what she was talking about, and she said, "I know what I'm talking about." I ignored her and told him I was pregnant, but the weird part was that I was saying it like I did something wrong. I was now feeling weird, what was going on here?

A few days later I was in so much pain, so we went to the emergency room, my husband came, his friend came, and that is when the doctor walked in and told me I was having an ectopic pregnancy and I was losing my baby.

I broke down crying and my husband hugged me in a cold, distant manner. My husband was feeling jealousy, but the truth was, I was dedicated to our marriage to our family, it was him pushing me away, it was him who kept mistreating me and now we lost our baby, and he was not emotionally with me.

Immediately after giving me a quick hug, he looked at his friend and said "come on let me take you home" we all looked crazy. How could he be worried about taking anyone home when we just lost our first baby together.

We all looked confused, but when I looked at his friend, he looked completely devastated. They left and I laid there alone and completely broken, I just cried and cried grieving the loss of my child. They kept me in the hospital for a procedure to help dissolve the pregnancy and my husband found reason after reason to leave and why he could not stay.

Again, I was alone. I called his friend from the hospital phone to check in after he left. He answered as if he was waiting for my call. I asked how things were over the loud music and sound of all the guys over his house as they did every weekend. He quickly told me he had been waiting for me to call and how upset he was with my husband.

He started telling me that I did not deserve the way he was treating me and then he said it "You deserve someone who is going to love you like the Queen you are!"

He continued to point out all the things he knew about me, I was a good mother, cook, wife, I was clean, and I loved so hard, and he was not okay with me being treated the way he witnessed. I thanked him and I tried not to read into it, but as the night progressed and we continued to talk he made it clear that he had been drinking and the alcohol started speaking for him.

He started confessing to me that he was feeling guilty but that his feelings for me had changed, he could not help but that he had different feelings, he was looking at me not like his little sis anymore but as a woman. Except this woman was not available. That call became awkward quickly.

In my mind I still only wanted to make things right with my husband, the one I vowed to love. But he was making that very hard.

This toxic relationship was always on an all-time high, and this time was no different. Things were just getting warmed up!

Chapter 13

Although I heard what he said, I honestly just tried to ignore it and blamed the alcohol. I had to let it go; I had bigger things to worry about. I was fresh home from the hospital, and the methotrexate shot they gave me to dissolve my pregnancy had taken a toll on me.

I couldn't eat, I was feeling sick because of the medication. It is very strong; it's given to cancer patients. I was five days without any food, I was losing weight at a very fast rate.

I felt like I was going through chemotherapy, my husband was so distant, and I was alone in my room when his friend called.He was calling to see how I was feeling and to check on my husband. We had lost our baby, and everyone was concerned.

 I was laying with the phone on my ear trying to stay still, so I wouldn't throw up. One of the side effects.My husband walks in the room and slaps me with his t-shirt across my face. I was taken back, what was going on? I just got slapped hard in my face with a shirt after just losing our child.

 He ran out the house, so I ran after him to see why he was acting this way and in front of my mother, my neighbors, and one of my daughters he yelled out "That's why you lost the baby because you're rotten inside!"

He should have just grabbed a knife and stabbed me in my heart, because those words hit like no words had ever hit me in my life, or were they?

How dare him talk to me that way, over an assumption, I wasn't doing anything wrong. I was completely broken. Nothing he said had ever hurt me or bothered me this way before. I was so hurt I could not even react. He knew me and knew that he better leave because I was a mad woman.

The next day I was looking out the window when I saw my husband outside getting high with the neighbor!He was back, and all I could hear was "You lost the baby because you're rotten inside!" I blacked out.

 I went into the hallway and grabbed a bat, my mother started begging me quickly, "Please you just lost a baby, you're so delicate, please think of your children, please!" I tied up my sneakers, grabbed my bat and ran down the stairs. Everything she said went in one ear and out the other.

 I snuck up on him and the words just kept repeating in my head, and I lost it. I swung that bat and hit him so hard on his leg and I knew I did damage, but he damaged my heart and now I was coming back for revenge.

The bat was just getting me warmed up, he was going to pay for those words. I called his friend and invited him to Philly. I needed to get away and he was ready. He got his daughter, his cousin, and we were out. We drove around Philly and the whole time I was thinking about them words over and over.

The closer we got back to Trenton, I could tell he wanted to talk but we were vibing, music was on, and everyone was just passing the blunt and enjoying the view. My mom started calling me blowing me up that my husband came back with a rage she had never seen.

He was breaking everything in my room, he even went as far as to urinate on my clothes, he was out for revenge too. He was on some heavy medications and blacked out. My mother called the police, and he was arrested that night.

I stayed out all night with his friend and his family. We talked all night, but I was still feeling the effects of the medication. The medication, the grief over the loss of my child, plus the words, oh, the words, they were killing me! Still, I was pretending to be okay.

 The next morning, I had my baby brother pick me up and I went to work with him. We were driving around doing deliveries when a detective called my phone, we needed to talk. My brother dropped me off to meet the detective in front of my house. As soon as he pulled up, he told me to turn around and put my hands behind my back. I was being arrested for assault with a deadly weapon.

My daughter was screaming, going crazy, begging the police officers to let me out. They were ready to arrest her! The way those police officers are back home, all I could do was beg her to calm down. I was afraid they would put their hands on her.

At that very moment I realized who I truly hurt when I picked up that bat, it was my daughter, and it was me. Here I was in Hamilton lock up, I had not eaten in five days, I was sick to my stomach, but I was here, and there was nothing I could do.

I was very respectful, so much that the officers let me sit on the phone all day and night.It was like God told them to let her get the phone, it is unheard of that you sit in jail with the phone between the bars sitting on your bed talking for hours.

My friend said, "I've been to prison for over 10 years, and I've never seen anything like this, you really on this phone like you're home!"

I really was on the phone like I was on my house phone though, and when I was not on the phone then I was sleeping. Anything to keep my mind off the fact that I was sitting in this jail cell with no shower, no hygiene products, this itchy blanket, no pillow, no food for six days, and to top it off, it was freezing.

I prayed to God continuously, especially when I found out in court, I was facing eighteen to twenty years.

After three long days my father sent the money to bail me out. I could have kissed the ground, my heart hurt looking at my mother and oldest daughter. Seeing them in court as they walked me in wearing handcuffs, I still can see the look on their faces as I stood before the judge.

I was home but the fact was I was still facing the rest of my life in prison, and I could not believe my husband and I were sitting a wall away from each other the last three days in jail. I was over it, once again he destroyed us for no reason. His insecurities, his mistrust, and the emotional abuse was too much.

I wasted no time after being released, I met up with his friend.He sat on the phone with me for three days while I was locked up, the whole time he was beyond himself that I was sitting in this place.He kept my mind going those three days we talked about everything, that is when he found out I loved to write not just to read.

That really blew him away, he made me promise I would read him something when I got out, and I assured him it would be my pleasure. Noone ever wanted to read my writings before. That blew my mind!

I was falling for his mind, and he was falling for mine too. The crazy thing, this was not revenge at all; my feelings were real.It was not hard to get myself caught up in this crazy situation since I was yearning for love, affection, attention, all the things this man wasn't giving me. This person though was more than willing to give me all these things I was in need for.

I was already feeling anger. It only grew when I came home and found out that the three days I was in jail, my kids were self-medicating off my medications to deal with the fact that I was in jail. My children could have died, and I was in jail. They found my high dosage anxiety medication and they were on the sofa dead to the world.

My mother was trying to hold everything together, but everything was out of control, and she was at her wits end. I came home and instead of realizing what my mother and my daughters and my second born son were going through, I was on a selfish road trying to feel loved.

Or was it selfish? I lost a baby and instead of a loving husband, I got a monster trying to break me while I was broken. I visited his friend that night and I could not do anything because I was still recovering from my loss but that night, he kissed me for the first time.

I was out for revenge, but he was out for my heart.

Things progressed quickly with us, he was reading my writings, we were on the phone for hours, I lost track of everyone around me, my entire world revolved around him.

I found out that he was involved with someone, but she was in a program for her drug addiction, and I did not care at the time because I was being comforted, so I thought. I was only fooling myself. I was falling for this man, and his mind but mostly I was falling for the way he loved me, the way he spoke to me, the passion he had for life and for me.

We were a power couple, we had plans to build an empire and every day we grew closer. I fell face first and hard, I could not believe it, I did not know what it was, but I knew I did not want it to end. Things got crazy when my husband found out about us. Now he thought we were doing him wrong all along, but we were not.

Things did not happen till after I came home from jail. He did not believe me, and he was out for his revenge. A vicious cycle that would continue for many more years.My husband called social services on me, and now I had these people in my house questioning me.

They were told that I got high, that I had no food, that my house was dirty, and whatever lies he could find to tell. They checked my house and quickly determined that it was all lies, my cabinets were full of food and my house was always immaculate.

Of course, I failed the drug test. I was getting high, I had been smoking weed my whole life to maintain myself, to keep myself from having to take the actual drugs the doctors were prescribing me that could cause me more harm than the marijuana.

I suffer from depression, anxiety, PTSD, panic attacks and I used the marijuana to deal with my mental illness but now I found myself in a program for drug addicts. One phone call to social services landed me in a rehab full of people who had serious drug problems, meanwhile I smoked some blunts to cope.I was now in a class learning about the reasons people go to drugs.

I was focused on revenge, on the fact that social services were called, when the reality was, God put me in that place. God had put me in that rehab so I could sit with that therapist to deal with all the things that were haunting me, since I was a child. It seemed that my story was even a lot for my therapist. I was learning so much about myself and my mental illness.

I did the things I did, felt the way I felt, and handled things in a way that had me waiting to see how long I would sit in prison for. I needed to be there. What the enemy thought was going to hurt me, God used it for my good.

It was the perfect timing, I was glad that I had the therapist, cause once again I was about to be broken hearted. This man sat me down to tell me how his girlfriend was about to come home from the program. Then he tells me that he had to go home with her, he needed time to explain things to her.

I was thinking okay, how much time? One hour, two, three? How much time? He did not have an answer. I was heartbroken, I was shattered. I could not believe that after finally finding love, it was being torn from me once again.

He told me how much he loved me, but I needed to understand that he lived his life by the rules. The rules where he had to be respectful because he was that type of guy. I tried to understand, but I couldn't! What about his loyalty to me? I gave everything up for him and now he had to be respectful!!

He might as well have pulled out a knife and stabbed me because that day he broke my heart. He cried and told me to just be patient and wait for him, that he would come see me every day and that he was going to fix it. He wanted to do it the right way, he did not want to be sloppy.

I was so angry! I was hurt. He came to see me every day like he promised, so I went along with it. He promised they were not being intimate, he just did not want her to be homeless since he was the only person she had in Trenton. I believed him, so I was compassionate. It was not her fault, and she should not be homeless, so I agreed to be patient.

It was fine at first, he told me there was nothing between them and that he was going to tell her the truth about me. I believed everything, then I prayed for clarity.

Immediately God answered, the girl was working for a temporary agency and in that temp agency worked someone I was close to. God has a way to show you the truth if you ask him to. If you need clarity, pray to God to reveal things for you and baby he will, quickly.

I got information from my friend that not only was this guy walking her to work every day and kissing her goodbye, but her neck was full of love marks. So, the whole time he was lying to me. He had no intentions on leaving her and if he did, he was not telling her that, instead she was being lied to, and so was I.

 While she was at work, he was with me. The news took me back, I felt betrayed, but I also felt like how could I expect God to bless my mess? I quickly ended things with him, I was not going to continue to get hurt and quickly I felt regret.

I had hurt my mother and my children and myself. How could I have been so naive, so vulnerable? I was drinking and getting high all day, I could barely function, I was at an all-time low. My friends were coming to check on me, my best friends, my brothers they both would come by to check on me and to push me to never give up!

 When everyone was gone, I was back to the anxiety and the desperation. We had a sofa on the porch and this day I was sitting on it just thinking about everything that was going on and I fell asleep outside on the porch. I was sleeping, like I was in my house in my bed no care in the world, or I was high? Either way I was awakened by my husband.

What was he doing here? I thought. He said he was walking by to see if he saw our children outside but instead, he found me sleeping. I was so angry with him; I was still facing charges.I had to go to this program every week and he was asking me if I was, okay?

 This man had nerves I thought, but I was so heartbroken and lonely I could use the company, so I let him sit. We quickly started talking and we smoked. We sat out there for hours just being honest about how we felt something we should have done a long time before that.

Again, vulnerable, and naïve, I ended up in bed with him. That night we decided to give it another go. I don't know what I was thinking? If he could go be with his girl, and break my heart. Then, I could get back with my husband and break his.

My husband, some friends, and I were sitting on the porch, when he pulled up in a car and asked to speak to my husband. They talked and they had a respectable conversation then he got in the car and left.

 I thought I would never hear from him again, but it seemed like that lit a fire in him where he wanted me back. Now he was calling me, showing up places, and telling me I was wrong for going back to my husband, but I was so angry with him I did not want to hear any of it.

Things between my husband and I were rocky, but we were trying to overcome everything. We kept pretending to be a happy family but deep inside I was dying. I was desperate. I felt like I could not breathe.

The holidays came by like they always do. For me they start in September with my birthday, then Halloween, Thanksgiving, Christmas, and New Year's! We were lit all those months; my husband and I were working hard to make it work.

I just wanted to keep smiles on my girls' faces, we had put them through so much. The whole family came over all my nieces, nephews, my baby brother, and all their friends for a New Year's party and it was one for the history books. We were so lit!!

It was all good vibes as if it would be the last party before a major change. We did not know at the time, but we were getting ready to make another major move.

I was determined to be loyal to my marriage because I knew that God was not going to bless me the way I was living. Although I had real feelings for this guy, I knew that I needed to try to get myself right.I would see him with his girlfriend and my heart would sink, it was making me depressed.

I found myself falling apart, even though he was still looking for me, I was not willing to play those games with him. I was never trying to have my cake and eat it too; I was honest with everyone all along.My husband knew how I felt, and he knew he had a lot to do with the way I felt.

He knew that he had neglected me for an exceedingly long time and now he was trying to make things right, so he said.Meanwhile he was still fighting his own demons because his mind was also playing tricks on him.

I found myself going back to the only place I knew to go when things were out of my control, the Bible.I was reading and praying, reading, and praying, I was begging God to help me stay loyal, to help me change, to help me get out of Trenton because I was dying, I could not breath!!I felt like I was suffocating.

I found myself one day clenching my bible to my chest looking out the window crying to God, begging him to find a way to please give me the funds to leave. I did not want to be there anymore, this was not healthy for me, my children, and especially not for my marriage.

This guy was not trying to let up and I was not trying to hurt anyone especially myself and he wanted to be with her and be with me.I was not doing that at all.

God heard my prayers, and he knew I was really trying, and he blessed my obedience. Not even a week later I got a check in the mail for thirty thousand dollars!!! Just like that!!!!

I bought a car, rented a U-Haul, packed it up, and the day came when we were going back to Florida. I cried thinking of how God did what he did!How I was waiting over three years for that money and without warning or notice it was there.

When I was desperate, when I needed it the most, when I cried to him begging him to save me, to get me out, he did. The U-Haul was ready. My husband was getting the last few things together with the kids and I ran out to the store to get some snacks and things for the long trip to Florida.

The guy found out I was leaving and he was not trying to let me go that easy. He showed up at my front door. My daughter opened the door, and she was scared when she saw him standing there knowing her daddy was upstairs.

She begged him to leave telling him her dad was upstairs and that I was not there. He told her to please tell me to go see him, not to leave that way!

My daughter just begged him to go! As a child she was terrified of what could go wrong! Something no child should ever go through. Fifteen years old and I knew she was smoking weed and getting into boys but that was the normal thing for a teenager, especially in Trenton.

I was not tripping over that. I just wanted my daughter to be honest and trust me with anything. My ex-husband dropped her off at a party with my permission. After not seeing them in six years, he was back around.

My youngest would not have anything to do with him, not because of anger, she felt that she did not know him. She met him when she was nine years old.

I tried to understand her, but I do not think I really did an excellent job. You cannot really understand something unless you go through it.

My husband was not happy at all that my daughter went to the party, and he warned me "If something happens at the party, it's on you!" For some reason I felt sick to my stomach when he said that. I would soon find out why.

My husband and I were sitting on the porch, and I had called to check on my daughter and my friend who was hosting the party, told me my daughter was fine. She was downstairs with her daughters, and I believed her.

I was enjoying the breeze with my husband on the porch, when I got a bad feeling. Soon after, my best friend calls me screaming! The house had been shot up, to hurry up and get my daughter!

I told my husband, and he gave me a look like he wanted to kill me, but instead he ran next door and got a ride from the neighbor. I didn't even get a chance to get in the car when they were gone. I begged someone else and got a ride behind them. I sat in the car shaking, I thought my heart was going to pop out my chest.

When I arrived, it was a scene out of First 48, yellow tape everywhere. I knew what that meant when my guy was murdered, I saw that same yellow tape. No, no, no!! I thought to myself, "where's my baby?" "where's my baby?'

I asked everyone I knew, there were people everywhere. Where did all these people come from and where was my baby?

My husband walked up on me, and I said where is she? where is she? Police were everywhere, the news was out there but I could not find my child.

I saw my friend's daughters outside but no sign of my daughter and no one was saying anything! In my life I had never felt so sick ever, I was feeling like I was about to die! Then suddenly, officers came out with my daughter in handcuffs.

I just started screaming, NO! NO! NO! NO! NO! NO! NOOOOOOOOOOOOOO!!!!!!!

The worst came to my mind. Did someone try her, and she was her mother's child, I raise my kids to defend themselves. Did she shoot somebody in self-defense?? What was going on? Why was my daughter in handcuffs and yellow tape?

Noone was telling me anything and I needed to get to the police station. Hamilton police had taken my fifteen-year-old daughter and would not tell me a word. I called my baby brother from the 7-11 on Lalor St. He came so fast, and we were out.

At the police station we sat out in the waiting room for hours without no answers, only questions. Finally, as we sat there full of anxiety and shaking, this girl came in with her mother and sat by us. The mom asked me if my daughter was the one in all black and I said yes, she asked me how my daughter is doing? I was even more confused, I told her I had no idea what was going on, no one had told me anything and that is when she told me everything.

My daughter was given Bacardi lemon earlier in the day, a fifteen-year-old girl who had no experience drinking, and she passed out drunk.

The girl told me how she had just met my daughter and that she had taken care of my child because she was so sick and laid her down in the bedroom next to the living room. This house was tiny, I was told it was a small party for about ten girls. They had put this event on social media and about 150 people showed up. They were charging at the door. Someone came in and shot up the party five people were shot.

When one of the gunshot victims got hit, he ran into the room where my daughter was out cold by the grace and mercy of God. He sat on the floor next to her and she never noticed. When the police came, they never cleared that room, which is right by the entrance of the main door.

When she saw the lights, she started waking up. She noticed the person was sitting next to her, so she started saying "Hey, wake up." She started moving him trying to wake him up and finally she called out "Hey someone come here he won't wake up!"

That is when police came in with all guns drawn, if that was not traumatic enough when my daughter looked down all she saw was the boy looking at her and blood everywhere. Police grabbed her, took her to another room, and put their hands on her as if she were guilty of something.

They took my minor daughter into an interrogation room without a parent and interrogated her for hours until the morning time. Even put hands on her trying to make her talk about whatever they thought she knew.

My daughter was drunk, asleep and woke up to a victim of a crime and became a victim to the police department herself. Instead of helping her, they made a bad situation into a worse one. My daughter would never be the same after that day. The pain in my child's eyes and the condition I saw her in, was more of a reason for us to make this big move and leave everything behind.

In Florida, my daughter would heal and have a chance to get past all this pain. I could heal from the loss of my baby since I never got the opportunity to grieve.Maybe, things could change for my family. It seemed that we could not catch a break. Now like myself, my daughter suffered from PTSD! We both had seen death face to face and now she would know what I lived with day in and day out.

My heart hurt for her, and this move was going to make everything better because that is what we do when things get hard, we run!! Right??

Chapter 14

As we crossed the Georgia/Florida border, we got a peep of the palm trees and all you heard was screams!!!! We were back home!!! We were so happy; it had been such a long time since I felt the peace I felt at that moment. Living in Trenton no matter how safe everyone told me I was, I never felt safe.

My daughters had watched someone get shot weeks before we left at the dollar general down the street. It was not only about my past, but it is also just the way things are back home, you just never know!

My hometown is really like that, we really go through real life situations! My people go through it, and nobody will ever understand the pain of the city unless you are from the city.It was so hard for me to leave home!

I really love my city, and I love my people back home, but I needed to go for my own mental health and the mental health of my children. We were driving on 95 like we had a destination, somewhere to go and we had none of that.

I had packed up, got on the road and did not even know where we were going. I had money, so I did not care. I had so much faith and trust in God that I told my family the same way God gave us the money, got us here smoothly, he will make a way for us!

I love how I told them, with confidence! When I talk about God, it must be with confidence, I really know he is going to do it! My God is really like that! Instead of worrying, I said, let's go eat!

Steak N Shake it was, we were in Jacksonville, FL. We ordered our food and my husband looked at me and asked, where were we going now?

 I asked them where they wanted to live. We lived in Florida before, could we go anywhere Kissimmee? Jensen Beach? Port St Lucie? West Palm Beach? Stuart?

They all chose Stuart so to Stuart we drove, four more hours and we arrived.

When we were leaving Jacksonville, I called my cousin in West Palm and told her I was in Florida, where I was and where I was going.She said I will meet you there! No hesitation she was there!We arrived in Stuart, and I was ready to get a hotel room for a week.

I could find a place and that was simple, but that was not God's plan for us.

There was not one room open in the whole city of Stuart or anywhere in South Florida. It was bike week and that week everything in the Treasure Coast was booked.

You cannot get a room except for the one we found that had bed bugs. It was always something with us. My cousin did not hesitate, we had been outside for hours trying to figure out what we were going to do. She said, "Let's go! You're coming home with me and you're going to stay with me until you find a place!"

 She was dead serious, and I knew that I could not say no, because unlike most people, she is the one who would always be there for you. No matter what, she will never turn her back on you. Her loyalty is unmeasured, and I love her to pieces. Today she has made me prouder than I could ever put into words, when everyone said she could not, she showed them she would!

She is what the definition of this cover is completely about, no matter how much this world takes, JESUS MAKES! I stayed with her for about a month or two and it was a blessing to spend time with her and my beautiful niece who I adore!

Every day we were going out trying to find a place, we went up and down West Palm and spent so much money on applications, but nothing would plan out. I was completely discouraged! I was sitting out by the lake, praying to God to help us get a place. I was so grateful to have a roof over my head and my cousin was a complete blessing, so I could not complain.

Still, I just wanted to get my things out of storage and into my own home. My oldest daughter was always so helpful, she was on craigslist when she found a house. When she showed me the house, it blew my mind! I had looked at this house back when we were in Jersey, more than once! It was far from where we lived, but could it be that I did not find a place here, because God wanted me there.

It was not a coincidence that it came up numerous times.I called the number listed and the property owner was amazing! We had the best conversation over the phone, we made an appointment for the next day to see the house.

 My daughter's and I jumped in the car and took the hour and a half drive to a town we had never been to before, but for some reason it kept coming up. When we were in Jersey my older daughter and I kept talking about this town, how cheap the rent was, how nice it looked. Also, when we were driving to Florida, we drove by it and my daughter jumped up screaming look Mami there it is! Vero Beach!

 Now after talking about it, driving by it, and talking about it again we were finally on our way to see what this Vero Beach was about!

 Soon we would see that it was no coincidence, but it was God working all things together for our good! We met with the landlord, and just like that, I was running to the bank to get him his money.

 I could move in the house in a week! God did it again! He found us the most peaceful town and the cutest house ever, simply perfect for us! I could not praise him more. I was beyond happy! I still can see my oldest daughter and I crying, jumping up and down hugging in the empty house. My baby has always been my backbone.God was in full control!

We enjoyed the next few days with my cousin and next thing you know it was time to go.We were so excited about meeting the property owner the next day, so we packed up and left the day before.

We parked by the beach, had lunch, and spent the day just thanking God, enjoying his marvelous works. All things in nature remind us how amazing the love of the father truly is. We were blessed.

I stared intently at the birds as they flew over the water, thinking how amazing God truly is! Soon I would be home. We spent the night at a rest area on 95 closest to our new house. Early in the morning we went to meet the property owner to get our keys and move in.

Thank you, Jesus was all we could say! Things were off to a good start, and we were settling in very well. The truth is, there was trouble in paradise!

It was about two months since we left Trenton, and I did not change my phone number so Jersey would call to ask me, why did I do this to him? How could I leave and break his heart?

But he was the one that had broken mines! Now it was too late. Years passed and the calls continued. We always kept in touch. Still, I always kept it a hundred with him, and kept my loyalty to my husband, but he never believed it.

My husband and I were never completely okay after the loss of our first baby. He never forgave me for being with Jersey either. To make things worse we lost four more after that first baby.

Our relationship deteriorated more with the loss of each baby. Through every loss, surgery, or procedure I would have to recover physically but also emotionally. I was not serving my husband as a woman and unfortunately that caused serious issues in our relationship and our marriage.

Now that I looked back, it had nothing to do with my recovery, it had everything to do with the past. The serious issues had never left.

All the things he had said and done to me, replayed in my head every day, and daily he thought about me being with Jersey. It was a recipe for disaster. Honestly, he should of never came back to look for me, especially when he only came back to torture me.

Every argument, every time something went wrong, he replayed the same song over and over. You slept with Jersey. Jersey, Jersey, Jersey!

He talked about him so much and bashed me for it year after year. I was tired of it; I was tired of feeling so bad about myself but still I stayed.

I believed I deserved that, I helped him punish me. I was calling myself all the same names he called me, I believed that was exactly who and what I was.

Every argument was the same song, repeating, I slept with Jersey, and he put me in jail. We lived in torment, the worst part of it all was my kids witnessed it year after year. It got so bad that they were imitating our behavior. There was absolutely no peace in this home.

I found myself praying to God, asking him to help me draw closer to him. He had done so much for me, and I needed him to heal me. I wanted to serve him and live my life right. Maybe this way I could be happy, maybe this way I could learn to love me and be worthy of love.

I believed for years that if I were good enough that he would forgive me one day and treat me the way I desperately desired to be treated. I was sitting in my room reading my bible when there was a knock on my door. It was the local Jehovah's Witness.

I was taken back, here I was praying to God for help, and they showed up! I quickly started taking bible studies and spending more time with the witnesses and trying to change my life. Every bible study was more like therapy to me, they wanted to teach me the bible, but I did not need that, I needed more.

My issues were emotional, I had a past that was holding me hostage, I had trust issues, I did not love myself, and I had deep generational curses all over me! I needed help. I would cry through every bible study, and I could tell she was aggravated with me. She tried so hard to help me, but you cannot understand something unless you have been through it.

Here I had been through so much and I needed way more than she or anyone could offer me, I needed God. I continued to go to the meetings and did everything to climb the ladder, you can move up from publisher to auxiliary pioneer, to regular pioneer and I just wanted to grow and serve God fully. For some reason I believed that I could get closer to God through hours.

I was finally an auxiliary pioneer for the first time in my life and I applied for a regular which only means you preach a certain number of hours a month. I wanted to give God 70 hours per month. He deserved it, but they denied me.

I could not understand. Why would you stop someone from doing more for God? They knew I was not ready. Although I did not see it coming, things started changing quickly.

I was doing everything right except for the fact that I always cried when it came down to God. If something touched my heart it would make me cry. I still cry when it comes to God, who would not? After all I have been through, how can't I cry when I think of the love of God, how good he is, and how good he has been to me. But no one could understand.

My husband and I were still having hard times, so I went to the elders to talk to them to get advice because I didn't want to mess things up more than they were.

I was very upset. I had so many things that I was carrying, years and years of pain and suffering on my chest. I broke down as soon as we got in that room, which I believed was a safe place. I believed that this was a hospital for the spiritually sick! The brother looked at me and said, "Oh the cry baby!" He was joking but those words were so harmful to me.

He could not even imagine how back those words would take me. When I was in Jersey, I heard a song at a meeting that touched my heart. I have been through some things, so if I hear about how good the Lord is, please do not mind me if I cry. After the meeting was over a sister said those same words to me "Oh the cry baby".

I remember cutting my tears short and getting up out of there so quick! There is no way I could make these people understand. I was not going to try today. I got in my car, and I drove away crying, as my kids watched.

Did they know how hard it was for a person like me to stay clean off weed, cigarettes, alcohol, sex and doing whatever I wanted to do to make the pain go away? Instead, I was here begging for God's help, crying to him! They had no idea about me.

They did not know how instead of driving my car into a tree, I came to the kingdom hall in the middle of the night and laid by the front door in the fetal position screaming begging for God to keep me alive and loyal to him.

They didn't know how I was feeling! Yet, they made me feel church hurt repeatedly. Every time I tried, they cut me deeper and I was tired.

My husband ended up leaving and they showed up at my house since I was not coming to the meetings after the "Cry baby comment" and I explained to them that my husband had left.

I had to find work. I was basically broke and stuck, they said that was too bad, shook my hand, and told me to call if I needed anything and that was the last time we spoke. I was over it; I couldn't do it anymore.

I quickly got some weed and a pack of Newport's 100s in the box and just like that, the old me was back. I was tired of trying and these people were basically mocking my love for God and my need for him, all they wanted was hours and perfection and I could not do any of it.

The part that hurt me, the worst was all the bible studies I left behind. All the people I was helping draw close to God!

Then I remembered what God said in his word, the job was already done. I had planted the seed, God would make it grow. He had it from there, they would be fine. Best part for me, he would never forget the works I did for his name.

I couldn't believe my husband had left and I couldn't work due to my mental illness, so I began hustling on the side doing whatever I needed to do to make it.

I found out I was about to be a grandmother and I was all my daughter had. If I had to make moves, then moves I was going to make. My father asked me to come to Puerto Rico for two weeks to get away because he knew it had been 27 years since I had been back.

I needed to get back to my roots close to my grandmother. There was something about the island that made me feel at home. My oldest stayed behind since she was early in her pregnancy and was really sick, so my mother came down to help take care of her while I went to P.R.My husband promised to come and help my mom while I was out of town.

I appreciated that although we were not together, we could still be cordial. That was growth.I was in Puerto Rico having the time of my life. I visited with my brother and his wife. It was a ball spending time with my nieces and great nieces. Taking my daughters around to see where we are from.

It is a special feeling to see their faces light up when they realize this is home and this is where our ancestors were brought. I always wanted my daughters to know their history to know who they are. After a few days in Bayamon, we went to the other side of the Island to Anasco to my Father's house.

I quickly took my daughters to see their Great grandmother's house! The corner house that always feels like home to me. I feel and always felt that's where I belong! My uncle was there, and my daughters finally were able to meet him. He suffered from alcoholism for every reason he lost a daughter and was never able to recover.

I never cared about that no matter where I saw him and no matter how many times, I always acknowledged him and always told him I loved him because I did. Who are we to judge anyone when we all need forgiveness and the lower the more worthy we are to Jesus?

My Aunt was also there, and we were able to talk, she was able to tell me some deep things that she carried in her heart. I knew exactly how she felt because I had felt the same feelings my whole life. We bonded in that living room in my grandmother's house, sometimes you cannot see how God is working but he is.

He took me there after 27 years to have those moments with my uncle because within a year he was gone. My God gave me the opportunity to say what I had to say after not seeing him in 27 years. I got to tell him I loved him and how much he meant to me, I was blessed with goodbye.

After an amazing trip I came home to enjoy watching my first grandchild grow inside my oldest daughter, nothing could ever compare.

I was so busy planning her ultrasound party, baby shower, and getting everything ready for the birth of my baby girl that I didn't even notice how my husband and I had teamed up to take care of our daughter and I allowed him back.

Even after he had come to my house with a neck full of what I call vampire marks. I was some kind of special, I tell you.

I lost my last baby two weeks before the birth of my granddaughter, she was born October 9, 2016.

My husband, my two youngest daughters, and I huddled around my oldest as we stared into each other's eyes full of tears.We welcomed our baby girl into the world! It was the best moment of my life. Everything was different, everything was okay.

A few days before we were running from a major hurricane, category 4. It was threatening to hit Vero Beach directly, but God was so good to us! My nephew left a bottle of shampoo and sneakers right in the middle of the yard, don't you know that the hurricane hit, and my neighbors lost power, trees came down, it was a mess but the sneakers and the shampoo in my yard did not even move!!!!!

Only God! Absolutely nothing happened to my house. I was truly blessed.As my granddaughter came into the world all I could do was exhale thanking God! He was too good!!!!!

I stayed the night with my daughter, we had the parents steak dinner together, and we bonded. She knew that no matter what, her momma was never going to leave her side!As I held my granddaughter, I promised her the same, Grandma will always be here for you, and I will never give up!

My mind was changing, I was not the same woman I used to be! Just that quick, I now had someone else I had to think about, Grandma's baby girl. My best friend was here.After the birth of my granddaughter the house was on cloud 9. This little girl filled our home with so much love, unity, and peace. She was all we needed to be happy.

Everything was going good when suddenly my daughter's dog bit the neighbor's dog and we got evicted.During the same time my daughter got kicked out of school. They sent her to an alternative school for "cursing at a teacher" ; the discipline just did not fit the crime. How could they put this child out? A child who gave no real problems, unlike my other two, just for cursing.

I had so much going on, we were about to be homeless again, and there were other things going on also, so I prayed. I remember telling God "Specifically" that although the discipline did not meet the crime, that if he had a plan for us and for my daughter that I would not make a fuss but allow him to take control.Something in my spirit told me he was up to something.

I got a call from the board. They were about to have a meeting and wanted to talk to me. I remember I was so down that day and the lady was confused as to why they would be kicking my daughter out for cursing and I told her with so much faith "God is in control, I know the crime and the discipline don't match but please don't look at that, pray before you make the decision and if you believe that my daughter can get the help she deserves at this alternative school, if she will no longer deal with the racism that we dealt with daily at this school, if she was going to be cared about and not judged for being Puerto Rican, loud, and dramatic then send her. Forget the crime and send her. I specifically told her to Pray about it and let God lead her"

She told me with a cracked voice, that I gave her chills and that she felt them words. When God is in the middle, nobody does anything about it!

My daughter was sent to the alternative school.What we thought was about her and her education, would turn out to be about God!About his plan and purpose for our life!

Don't ever underestimate God; he is a very organized God, and he can use any situation for his purpose. My daughter and I showed up for our appointment so we could meet with the staff and get her going.

I walked in there one way, but I left that school another! Our lives would never be the same after that day.

Chapter 15

My daughter and I arrived for our appointment; I had a bad taste in my mouth for the school system. Since we arrived from Jersey, I had been fighting for them to understand what they did not know.

Being from Jersey we had our own way, and it was a way that would not be accepted in this small town. We came here for peace and now we had a different war we were fighting. I immediately sat down, and I waited to be greeted but that never happened.

I wondered how they wanted the children to have manners and be polite, but the adults were not leading by example. I could not hold it in.

I was angry, bitter, and ready to lay them out. I walked up to the desk, and I let the receptionist know how I felt. If they want the children to change then we as adults need to lead by example.

The adults should greet people, as they arrived, it was the polite thing to do. The principal quickly came out!

If I was ready, I met my match because he was ready too! Not the way you think. He would do it with love. The principal quickly took my daughter and I back and apologized for the way I felt. I say "felt" because sometimes "WE FEEL" we are right. When we are so far from the truth.

 The pain we carry does not allow us to see the truth, all we see is how we were wronged, then we walk around wronging others just because they remind us of what originally caused us pain.

 Hurt people, hurt people. But God!

 He was so on time, that the principal sat us down and listened to us. From the injustice at the school, to how church hurt we were, to the neighbor suing my daughter for her dog biting hers, and now we were about to be homeless, he heard it all.

He felt compassion. It was so clear for the first time in a long time someone cared. He told us "I am not only the principal here, but I am also a Pastor at a church. I would love for you all to come by sometime!" Then he stood up, grabbed my daughter and I by the hands and prayed for us like no one had ever prayed before. I walked into that school desperate, anxious, and depressed, I walked out peaceful! The peace of God had come over us both!

My daughter and I just stood there looking at each other wondering what just happened?

We had a few days left before we had to be out the house and I could not help but to think about the prayer earlier in the day, as anxiety was trying to creep back in.

Quickly I remembered the peace I felt after the prayer, so I prayed to myself and asked God to please help me see him and help me trust him. My God!!!

The next morning, I dropped my daughter off at her new school where I knew the Pastor/Principal was going to be a blessing in her life. One prayer and he had already blessed me. I was so grateful to God that she would be able to be in a place where she could get the help she so desperately needed. My kids had been through so much and my heart hurt for her.

As I was driving back home, out of nowhere, it was as if my car made a left all by itself. It was crazy. A small for rent sign on the corner and let me just say that I am blind! How I saw it and turned at the last minute, was like God shaking me up saying "wake up, pay attention."

I drove to the end of the street and the last house on the left was for rent. I immediately called and the landlord asked me to meet her there in the afternoon and I agreed. I arrived on time to meet the landlord and she told me and another lady who was there to do a walk through and to come talk to her when we were done.

I immediately was taken back; this house was beautiful. So beautiful that I couldn't imagine her renting it to me. My brain immediately told me "The other lady is getting it because of the way she looks" but let me tell you how wrong I was!!!

This house had a sign that said, "ONLY GOD!!!" Only God can take the seven things you loved about the last seven houses you saw and put them all into one!!!!! I could not believe it!

 It explained why none of the last seven applications went through! God had for me what I couldn't even imagine for myself. I stood in the yard looking up at the sky, I could love living here. I went inside and I noticed the landlord was having a conversation with the other lady so I went out back again and took another look at the sky and asked God to do his will.

As I stood there silently the landlord came up behind me and said, "It's beautiful right" and I quickly agreed. She asked me, what I thought about the house? I excitedly responded, "I love it!!" Then she asked me how long I wanted to rent the house, and I told her until I buy my own home. That's when she told me she was a realtor, and that she would love to help me when I was ready. After an amazing conversation she told me to give her a few days until she made her decision.

It was the longest wait ever, but I finally received the text that the house was ours we could move in! Hallelujah Lord you did it again!!!! We were so happy to move into this beautiful house with these huge French doors that looked amazing with the high ceilings. The house was just gorgeous, we were so blessed.

It was a joy to see my granddaughter playing on her playmat on the hardwood floors in her and her mommy's new bedroom. I couldn't even believe how God had showed up and showed out.

 The next Sunday I was determined to go to that church. How did I find this house the morning after the pastor prayed for us to find a home? I had to go see what was going on at that church.

Sunday morning arrived and I was feeling confused. How could I go to another church when I was raised as a Jehovah's Witness? If I even dared walk into this church, I would be labeled an apostate. As someone who serves another God, my family would really disown me. My mother would never talk to me again, but still something was calling me.

So, I dressed my granddaughter and I got myself ready and we got in the car. I had no gas and no money either, the yellow light was on. I was on E and the church was a good twenty minutes away from my house. I sat in the driveway debating should I stay, or should I go, so I made a deal with God.

I prayed and I said "Jehovah if you want me to go to this church and there is something there that you want me to hear, then you will get me twenty minutes with no issues safe and sound. But if you are against me going to that church and you feel that I am going against you and your son Jesus Christ in any way, then leave me and my granddaughter stranded on the side of the road on the way there!" I turned on the car and by faith I started our trip to the church.

After a peaceful, relaxed twenty-minute drive, we arrived at the small white church that could be in a Madea's movie. It was adorable.

St Matthew's Missionary Church, the first church I would step foot into, but I knew that God was okay with me going. He had something there for me because I did not break down. I walked in and immediately I could hear the choir singing and I was blown away I had never seen anything like it before.

I had never witnessed people worshipping God this way except for movies but this was no movie, this was real life, and I couldn't help but to stand up out of my chair with my granddaughter in arms and start clapping cause this church was lit!!!

After the choir finished singing and the pastor preached a good word, I remember him saying if you believe in Jesus and you want everyone to know then come up to the altar. I just looked around and I just stood up and ran up there cause of course I believe in Jesus…

I didn't know it was an altar call, I had never been at a church before, so I was so lost. But I knew I believed in Jesus. The pastor came and talked to me, and I just remember telling the church how hard it was for me to be there. I was raised a witness, and this would cause me a lot of harm.I told them that I knew I was supposed to be there because of my deal with God.

I told them how God did not let me break down but instead he got me there. The pastor prayed over me and asked me if I wanted to get baptized? I was already baptized, at twenty-one.

After so many sins if he would baptize me again then I would be willing to. He told me that next Sunday, it would be my baptism and I agreed. I sat back down so happy knowing that something was happening in my life, that God was back amid it.

As I sat there listening to the rest of the church, a woman walked up to me and put something in my hand. I did not dare to look, then another person, and then the pastor came with an envelope.

I arrived there with no money and left there with eighty dollars for gas and food. I was taken back by God and how he took care of me that day. I was truly amazed! As my granddaughter and I drove back I couldn't stop thinking about the goodness of God and how he had blessed me so abundantly with a home and now he had given me my daily bread.

I couldn't wait to come back to church, that praise and worship was it for me. I needed some more of that in my life. I had recently started listening to gospel music and I just blasted "grateful" on the radio and enjoyed the peaceful ride back to Vero Beach.

I could feel it in the atmosphere. My life was getting ready to change once again. I started going to church faithfully and I was still hustling to make ends meet so it was interesting when people would come over now, they wouldn't hear the normal Black Youngsta or Styles P. Now they were hearing Tamela Manns and Marvin Sapp and even they were being blessed by it.

It started endless conversations about God and what he was doing for me. Quickly they knew it was real, I told them they were welcome to visit as friends, but I would no longer be serving them. I couldn't eat from both tables, and I had to trust in God to provide for me and that's what I did.

I enrolled in school and for the third time I was attempting to become a Medical Assistant, the second time was when I was in Georgia I quit when we left abruptly to Florida and ended up in bed with the fleas.

I had also lost my associates degree that I was going to be handed, after my last class which was CPR. I had completed a two-year degree but right before I moved, they lost their accreditation and I lost everything. Now I was back at it. Third time a charm they say, well I was praying they were right!

I went down to a local agency called the EOC and I applied for a scholarship to go to school. After intense interviews and a workshop I was chosen to receive a full paid ride to finally accomplish one of my biggest goals!

I looked at my granddaughter and I said, "This time baby I am going to do it and Grandma is going to do it for you!" Life was good. I was making so much progress after five long cries at the altar and the powerful men and women of God praying over me.

I was finally moving forward from the past that had haunt me for so long. God had his hands all over me, I started making changes, and progressing spiritually rather quickly.

I could tell the growth, even when there was a woman at the church who would go out of her way to make me feel uncomfortable. I ignored it and continued chasing the feeling that I got every time the spirit would move in that place.

I was blessed with joining the choir and I even started speaking from the pulpit. God continued to bless me in every aspect of my life. I was doing amazing in school, and I even took a part time job in the laundry at a local nursing home.

I was so busy, but I felt completely fulfilled. I had never felt this level of accomplishment before. I was so focused. I was going to school in the morning, working after school, then I would be up until three or four in the morning doing homework and studying to be back up in the morning to do it all over again.

In between, I enjoyed every minute with my beautiful granddaughter. I was determined to go hard for my girls and my granddaughter. I kept telling myself don't forget who's watching and I ran with that.

I was experiencing God in a way that I had never experienced before. I didn't know anything about praise and worship, speaking life into my life, feeling the holy spirit, none of it. I was raised to worship God in a very subtle way, and this was far from subtle.

I was learning and growing spiritually and then like clockwork things went left, my mom got wind of my baptism and my newfound faith at the Baptist church. Immediately her and all my Jehovah's Witness family and friends cut me off, I was heartbroken.

 I couldn't understand how me serving the same Jesus they served would cost me this tremendous loss.

So much time passed and still no word from my mother, it was the longest I had ever gone without talking to her and I was feeling so discouraged but I was still fighting. I remember we had a revival at church, and I was there and ready.I showed up with an expectation!

I was expecting a word of encouragement and the joy I felt whenever I was on that pulpit singing with my sisters! I was down, but I knew that God was in control and my faith was at an all-time high! Never did I trust God, the way I trusted him now! He was made so real to me, so active, and so powerful!

They taught me that God was working actively now, not only in the future! That night I knew that to be the truth! We had a guest pastor, and everyone was saying how amazing she was. I couldn't wait to hear her preach. Immediately she went into praising like no other before, you could see the love for Christ from across the room.

 It was real, her love for God was the truth. I knew by her praise that she had been through some things. You can only have praise when you have seen God during your storms. I knew her praise all too well because I felt it inside of me.

God had been so good to me, even though I was feeling so much pain from hurting my mother, but only if she could understand and see for herself the love we all had for God too! The pastor began preaching and it was on point!

Out of nowhere she stopped and walked across the room. She said the spirit led her there. She started prophesying over a sister's life and telling her very specific things about what she was going through and that sister just broke down in tears. I was shocked because I had never seen that before.

She walked over to maybe two more people and spoke to them and then out of nowhere she stopped and said, "wait a minute, wait, the spirit is leading me over here!"

Over here was getting closer to my direction rather quickly. The pastor walks up to me and just looks at me with this look of love, compassion, but hurt like she saw right through me. She said "Baby, you've been through so much, so, so much, and all your life you've been hurting, but God loves you so much."

Then she says, "I know things are bad with your mom" I immediately began to cry. How did she know about that? I don't know her from a can of paint. She continued, "But don't be discouraged, your mom is going to call you sooner than you think." Then she came close and whispered in my ear, "You're going to get a big check, I don't know from where, or when but baby you're going to come into big money and when you do you will know, because of how substantial it will be. You're going to come back and testify."

I looked at her with eyes full of tears and said, "I receive it right now in the name of Jesus!" A few weeks later she was coming back to the church, and I told my husband, "Listen you need to come to church, you have to come listen to this pastor she is the truth!" He agreed and we went. We decided to sit at the farthest end of the church way in the back. He wanted to hide since I told him about my experience, he didn't want to be seen.

Everything was going well; she was preaching a good word and then it happened. She was led to the opposite side of the room and was speaking to others when it happened. Just like last time, she stopped again and said "wait, wait, wait I gotta come over here!

This time we were way in the back, there was no way she was talking about us. Boy was I wrong! The pastor walked all the way around the church to the back where we were hiding, but this time the message was for my husband. That same look of hurt she had I saw again.

She looked at him with so much compassion and said, "Wow! Baby you are suffering so much, you can't sleep at night because of the nightmares, right?" The difference was my husband didn't go to church like I did.

He randomly visited and she never met him. I never told anyone about his nightmares or our past so how did she know? That was the moment of impact, the holy spirit was real, and it was working through this woman of God!

Then it got deeper, she said "You've been running for your life for a while, they've been trying to kill you for a long time and that's why you're having nightmares! But God came to tell you that you will not be killed, you will live and not die! Your nightmares are gone AS LONG as you put God first in your life!" Then she got the anointed oil and not like she did the rest of us, a small amount on our forehead, no, no, no!

She POURED the oil on the top of his head in a large amount and said that the spirit told her it had to be done this way. She prophesied over his life, she said "You will be a pastor one day in the name of Jesus! You will be speaking in front of many bringing them to Jesus!"

I jumped up and cried out loud! I received it! I claimed it in the mighty name of Jesus! After that day his nightmares went away! The thing was, she made it clear, ONLY IF he looked for God would these things be.

About a month had passed by and Hurricane Maria was taken over Puerto Rico and had destroyed so many islands in her path. It was heart wrenching to watch! As I sat there out of nowhere just as the women of God said it would happen, the phone rang, it was my mother. My mother was concerned about our family in Puerto Rico and I was her contact with them, so she used the situation at hand to reach out to me. I was so elated, quickly I praised God!

He spoke to the woman of God to calm my anxiety, to give me hope and to build my faith so that I could endure and most importantly he quickly came through like a champ, it was done!! Not long after that, my mother called and was very upset that things weren't going well between my sister and her. My mother was living with my oldest sister and granted our mother is not easy to deal with by far, but it broke my heart to hear her upset about the situation.

My mother had moved out and was staying with a friend and that did not sit well on my spirit. I knew I was pushing it since she had just started speaking to me, but I asked her anyway. "Mom, come with me please, I would love to have you here and you can meet   your great-granddaughter!"

My mother agreed and packed it up and came to live with me in Florida. God had stood on his word, he made it happen for me. My mother was back home with me after so many long years. I couldn't be happier! I was so looking forward to sharing my changes with my mother.

 How I was living a life that would make her proud. I was serving God full heartedly, God had blessed me with this beautiful, comfortable home. I was working, and still in school with a 4.0 GPA. I could finally make my mother proud I thought!!

Chapter 16

Things were great in the beginning of mom's arrival. I loved watching her and my granddaughter, as they walked hand in hand, my heart was full! My mother showed me compassion as she watched me work so hard. School, work, homework.

I was helping with my granddaughter, so my daughter could go to work, and keeping up with a house full of older teenagers was far from easy.My mother noticed. I would get home from working in the laundry late at night, and my beautiful mother would be up waiting for me.

I would immediately sit at my desk to get to that homework, because I knew that GPA wasn't going to keep itself up. My mother would ask me if I was hungry and fix me something if I was. I appreciated her so much. I was so happy having her there. The prophecy had come true.

The holidays were approaching along with my graduation, and I couldn't be happier knowing my mother would be there to see one of my biggest accomplishments! Unfortunately that wouldn't last long either.

My granddaughter's father surprised us one night with a huge Christmas Tree and all the decorations, it looked amazing!That did not go very well with my mother being a Jehovah's Witness. Her attitude started changing immediately and I could see that she was not happy at all. I felt bad, I really did. I didn't want anything but for my mother to be with us and be happy. At the same time, I was not going to allow my granddaughter to miss out on all the things that my kids and I did.

 This time I was not going to waiver. My graduation day came, and I could not be happier. I was surrounded by these amazing women who had been through this long journey with me! Women who like me were up all night and up all day to get to this point where we stood in our Royal blue! I could not pick a better group even if I hand picked them myself!

 We had become a family and tonight we were celebrating this huge accomplishment together, in front of our family and friends, I was on cloud nine. I was even more excited since I was going to receive the highest award in front of my mother,

 I was Valedictorian of my class, and it was so huge to me because I was one of the oldest in my class and a grandmother! I was also a high school dropout. I was someone who had every reason to quit, to fail, and instead I came back after failing twice with a vengeance! I nailed it! Never give up!

I was a nervous wreck when they called me up to give the class speech. It was a privilege and an honor that I was so grateful to be receiving. I got to the mic and immediately I gave all the praise and all the honor to my heavenly father because it was only him that sustained me all of them days and all of them nights.When all I wanted to do was crawl in bed, quit, and give up, GOD never let me!!!!!! His plan for me was never to fail! It was always to win!

 I was so blessed to share that moment with my mother, and to put my certificate in her hands with the words "VALEDICTORIAN" on it! It was one of the biggest, happiest moments of my life. My Pastor and our First Lady were there to support me, as well as my husband, my daughters, friends, and of course my amazing EOC family who no doubt were the reason I was able to accomplish so much!

After an amazing celebration at Ay Jalisco's, we drove home to rest after a long journey. Tonight I could sleep without thinking about homework, school, none of that. Tonight, I was getting some much-needed rest and that's exactly what I did.

I was awakened by the sounds of my phone ringing. I must have been dreaming that I graduated, and I was late for school. I answered quickly as if I was already up, "Hello?" My teacher quickly said, "Are you ready to work?" I was confused, I just graduated yesterday, a job not even 24 hours later.

Could this be happening? It was!! I got the job and started as a medical assistant for a local pediatrician.I was excited! I was so grateful to my God because I was the first person out of my class to be offered a job and it was only God who could do something like that for someone like me.

 I quickly realized that I could apply for my dream job now and quickly I did. After a few months, I was on lunch break looking out at the boats, when out of nowhere I got a call. It was Lawnwood, the trauma hospital, finally, finally!!!! After all this time I was finally going to live my dream!! I was hired and just like that I was a phlebotomist at the trauma hospital in Ft Pierce and things were about to get real!

In my imagination, I would be taking blood from the sick and I would be going to hospital rooms and drawing some blood, boy was I wrong. I quickly realized on day one of training that I would be drawing blood from every unit of the hospital, including all the ICU'S.

This meant TICU which is a trauma intensive care unit. Also, I would be going to every trauma when they were called, code blues, and everything that you are not mentally prepared for when you start your first shift at a trauma hospital. My trainer was no joke, she is what I call a veteran and knows her stuff, but she did not play.

We clicked so well, I was enjoying my time with her and our conversations but mostly I was enjoying how much she was teaching me about getting the blood. At one point she shared her opinion about how she felt about another co-worker. That was fine, I am a good listener.

The problem started when I was introduced to that co-worker, the both of us also instantly clicked!I am a people person, I love people, so there was enough room for both co-workers.

Their relationship did not have to be "OUR" relationship. Unfortunately, my trainer did not feel the same way. I still look back and wonder... maybe she thought I told the girl what she confided in me? I never repeated a word she said forward.

Although she had her own opinions about the girl, me and this girl hit it off. I love to joke with her and tell her it was love at first sight! The energy between us was so strong we couldn't help it; you would think that we were friends all our life from day one we were inseparable.

We could not wait for our next hot tea session!We were too busy talking about our own lives to be worried about others. Plus, my life alone was all the hot tea we needed.

I was not at the "Wood" for a full two weeks, when we got a code blue. My trainer and I immediately arrived. I quickly realized how real my job was, but it was about to get as real as it could get, quicker than quick.

The nurse who was performing CPR was visually tired and everyone else was working hard trying to get the patient back to life. The nurse started calling for backup. Someone needed to take over CPR but there was no one, and it just came out "I'm certified ".

Immediately I caught myself and realized I had never given CPR to a live person. I had just volunteered myself and there was no turning back. I expected a no, surprisingly she said hurry up get in! I ran over there, and it was the most natural thing that I started giving CPR for the first time to a real human.

I remember watching the screen looking at each compression, praying for him to come back. I pushed and pushed on his chest and then his family walked in and that's when it really hit me. His life was in my hands, and they are watching me for a sign of hope, and I could not give it to them. He passed away.

It hurt me to my core, but you learn quickly in that setting that there is no time for emotional breakdowns when you have other lives that need to be saved. You just had to keep it pushing. I worked the graveyard shift so when six thirty hit I drove home in a puddle of tears, thinking of the life that was lost in my hands early that morning.

If the pressure at work was not enough, I had plenty more at home. Four years had passed, and things were not better, everything just kept getting worse and worse. My daughter was still dealing with the aftermath of the trauma she endured.

 She was fighting through life with so much anger and pain that it was difficult for her to move forward but she still managed to. My daughter graduated from high school and completed a CNA course together with her older sister. I was blessed to see my daughters follow me into the medical field.

We were cheering and pushing each other to be successful!

I remember this morning like it was yesterday, my middle daughter had to be at work, and she needed a ride. My daughter knocked on my door and asked me to take her. I was so tired that day, I was not getting sleep due to me working so much. I was exhausted.

If I could go back to that day, I promise I would jump out of bed and go take my baby to work, the decision I made changed our lives forever.

I was so irritated with her because she would have rides everywhere, this girl would never be in the house all the time, but when she needed important things done, it was always me who had to show up.

That morning I was over it. I caught an attitude and asked her why her friends could not take her? A decision I still regret. Sometimes you do not realize all that your children have inside, how much pain they are carrying around. So many ugly situations they have lived through. many because of decisions I had made. That day was her breaking point.

I look back and I can imagine what she felt. She was doing everything right, even though she was exhausted emotionally. She had been through so much without any denying it, and that was the moment it showed.

My daughter began to scream and yell, she even cried as she went crazy in that house. She mentioned how I would do anything for my husband, but I made it so difficult for her! I ran out and tried to calm her down because I could honestly see the pain in my child's face and it was not about respect at that moment, it was about the pain she was carrying that I was not aware about.

About the fact that she had woken up to a dead body and was traumatized, instead of the only father she knew comforting her, he stopped talking to her for days. Only because she was hugged up with a boy at the party and he found out. I could not make any sense of his way of reacting to real life situations.

This day wasn't any different, instead of him staying in the room and letting me handle the situation, which was the reason I walked out and closed the door behind me. He began going off in the room calling my daughter out her name and cursing her out like she was a total stranger.

Then he called the police as I begged him not to, to please let me handle it that my older daughter was going to take her to work and to just let it go. He did not. One ride cost my daughter her career, my daughter would go from a CNA to a felon in a matter of minutes.

The police arrived so fast, and my husband went out and immediately told them he wanted my daughter out of the house and that killed my daughter! It killed me. My daughter is the most loving person you will ever meet but that same daughter, just like her mother, will become your worst nightmare if you hurt us. My daughter immediately spit in his face.

This is the worst thing anyone can do to you, he had spit in my face, now she was repeating what she saw, learned behavior. She was now spitting.The years of watching him and I fight, the times we slept in the car, the times he was acting crazy in the house, and we were scared!

The Christmas tree I had destroyed, the knives they saw getting pulled out, and all these years of domestic violence between my husband and me. Also, between their biological father and I, all the pain was coming out! He asked the police if he was going to arrest her for spitting on him and the officer who had no intentions before, quickly slammed my daughter into our concrete porch.

My youngest daughter lost it, she disrespected the only father she ever knew for the first time in her life, the officers slammed her down too!

 I cried and begged the officers to please let them go, to please give us a chance to fix this. I desperately begged them, just to be told by him "Are these the types of animals you raised? You should be ashamed of yourself!" I was degraded again.

I ignored him and quickly ran chasing them as they walked my two daughters in handcuffs to the back of their car.

My daughter, dressed in her purple uniform, was now that scared fifteen-year-old who woke up to a dead body, the same girl police arrested, beat, and interrogated without thinking how that would affect the rest of her life.

No excuses for how she behaved that day!She was not my beautiful blue-eyed child who was full of love! The person who would give anything to help anyone.The girl who loves senior citizens, and taking care of special needs children. This girl loves harder than anyone and she was a stranger. That girl in that moment was what insanity looks like.

I witnessed it with my own eyes. That should have never happened. I can still see myself standing in the road as my baby screamed and kicked in the back of that police car knowing that this is what I had caused. It felt like everything was spinning and I was just stuck there.

The officer was right. I should be ashamed of myself, not my daughter, not her behavior, but myself for not putting God first, for failing God, for allowing myself to fall back into the pit. I stood there crying but not long because there was no time for that, I had to get my baby out!

I had to wait until the next day to get her bailed out. It was Sunday and I worked overnights, so I had just enough time to make it to church before I had to meet with the bail bondsman who was coming in just to help me out.

I got to the church, and I was beside myself, my life was a wreck, but I was still holding on to the hem of his garment. I remember I was still in my uniform, that's how crazy things were, but still I managed to go where my present help was.

I arrived and as soon as I felt the spirit moving the tears just began to fall, I had to hold on! I could not lose faith, even if my baby was in that jail cell, even if everything had fallen apart, I had to hold on!

That is when the enemy always comes to do what? STEAL, KILL, AND DESTROY!!!!!!!

A sister comes to me and looking back now I tell you Satan will walk into the house of God and sit next to you in church just to make you leave our father, especially when we need him the most!!!

Back to the sister, she tells me "You know it's not good to always be crying like that!" I went from crying to an immediate straight face, and with a broken heart I looked at her and told her "Church is a hospital for the sick, and that's why I am here right now. My baby is sitting in jail, I just worked ten hours, my marriage is in a wreck, and I came here to get help, and you just discouraged me. I pray you don't do that to anyone else!" and I walked out!

I could not even think on the way to the bails bond! It was a full attack on my spiritual life and Satan was not even ready to let up! I got my daughter out and she was different, she was hurt and angry! She cried, "Mom I am charged with a felony, I just lost my career mom!"

I had no words to say as I dropped her off because she could not even come home. There was a restraining order from her coming near my husband. This was a nightmare I was living. I had that sick feeling again.

Our marriage was already in shambles because of the situation with our daughter and things were just going to get worse! My oldest daughter also moved out with my granddaughter.

I felt like someone ripped my chest open and pulled my heart out and smashed it right there in front of me. How could this be?

I have had my granddaughter by my side since the moment she was born. Now I would be forced to live without the early mornings, our afternoon nap, my baby girl running to me when I got home from work, and I was not even ready.

I felt like my world was coming down crashing right on top of me. Why now? How did things change so suddenly? When my daughter moved out the truth that was already creeping at the door became known quickly.

The only thing that was holding our marriage together was our granddaughter. We had lost five babies of our own; the last one was two weeks before our Babygirl was born, and we were broken. Our granddaughter was filling a void in my husband's life.

He has never had his own biological children. After losing five with me, my granddaughter gave him something he needed.

I understood, but unfortunately my husband had a habit of shutting completely down every time things got rough, and he was in a dark place. Since my granddaughter was born, he was not that way, he had changed.

We would go out all the time, we were a family for the first time. That baby filled our house with so much love and joy, she was everything each one of us needed. The moment they left everything changed.

My husband was in a dark place since we all blamed him for my daughter being arrested and losing her career. This was something even until this day I know, should have been dealt with in house. Things had changed overnight; I no longer knew him.

We were living two completely different lives. I was pushing my way through church, crying, and hurting through every prayer call. I felt like I was losing the battle and losing myself in the process.

The more I tried the worse things got. Although I wanted to save my marriage, I could not live with knowing the man I was laying with had my baby arrested. I did not trust him.

Things had gotten so crazy, In between the church hurt, and my marriage you could see that I had fallen back to a place I was so far from. I was back to smoking weed; it was the way I have always dealt with anxiety.

I ran back which quickly led back to cigarettes which were always at reach since my husband had never left our old life behind. But that was not it, things were just getting interesting.

Chapter 17

My oldest daughter was now pregnant for the second time, and it was exactly what the family needed to try to bring everyone together. My cousin's wife, who I consider more than a sister and I planned a gender reveal and we couldn't have been more excited!

The house was full of our friends and family. We all went out back to wait for the pony, would it be a boy or a girl?

We nervously waited; everyone knew I wanted a boy!

I had three daughters and now a granddaughter. I would be happy either way, but I was hoping for a boy. Finally, after what seemed like forever, the pony dressed in pink came around the corner, I lost it!! I ran and screamed!!! I forgot about the boy thing so fast, my granddaughter was on the way!!! I could not be happier!

That would change by the end of the night. My husband left the party early. He came to me to say he was leaving; I could feel his energy was off. Things had been rocky for so long I didn't pay it any attention. Maybe I didn't even care.

I was done cleaning up and finally sitting down to relax, when my daughter called. She was sitting, watching my husband with another woman at the local 7-11.

I was pissed. A day when our family was supposed to be together celebrating, he managed to ruin it for me as he did for most holidays. I couldn't remember many times when he surprised me. I realized at that moment; this was the same man who froze when it was time to say his vows to me. This was the same man that still after thirteen years had not bought me a wedding band.

But still I was holding on to a dream, but that is what it was. I quickly confronted him and of course he denied everything and said that my daughter was lying. Something he knew a lot about. I knew my daughter was not lying because she had forgiven him for getting her locked up. Even though she had an upcoming court date.

Me and him had a huge fall out and he moved out. He made himself the victim stating that I had made him homeless, which was not the first time this happened. I always believed if you could ride with other women and spend time with them, then you can stay with her too!

I was so hurt, why now that I was giving everything to him, to our marriage, to our kids he would hurt me this way again. But he did, and I would do what I always did, I got caught up with someone else trying to find healing for my heartbreak.

This time I crossed a line I said I would never do. That's why you should never say never because you never know where you will be.

I got involved with a married man, he knew me and my situation and most importantly he knew my love for God. I will never blame anyone for my decisions, but God knows I had no intentions to cross any boundaries.

I thought I had found someone I could trust and someone I could talk to. Someone who was able to help me grow and lead me in the right direction. I fooled myself, I found myself in an uncomfortable situation that I should have ended that very moment. I knew better, and I knew I was not comfortable with the situation at all.

Instead, I allowed the calls to continue and allowed myself to be convinced that because this person had everything, he was a good man. I imagined that he would change my life, what a fool I was.

Instead of learning to love myself for once, I again was looking for someone else to validate me, to make me feel loved, and to take away the pain that I was feeling. I started letting the trips, the name brand purses, and the money make me forget about God, my morals, my standards, and the fact that my daughters were there watching.

Hurt people hurt people.

It did not take too long for me to come to my senses. He sent me on a trip to Jersey. Things were rocky between us so he thought it would help.God ain't gonna bless no mess!!

I went to Jersey, and I remember talking to my niece, and it was weird because she is not the niece I would normally talk about things of this nature, but GOD!!!!! My spirit pushed me to talk to her about my situation and how convicted I was feeling.

I knew she was a spiritual woman, she would give me the RIGHT advice!

My niece sat quiet for a minute, and just like that she said, "God told me to tell you, go back home and tell that man that if he doesn't stop doing everything that he is doing he will lose everything he has, and you cut all ties immediately!"

The hairs on my arms and the back of my neck went up because this was not the first time my niece had prophesied; God had used her many times before and he did it again!

I had to meet with him when I arrived, to return the car rental he got me. He got in the passenger seat, and I got straight to business! I was not playing with God!

I immediately told him what my niece had prophesied over him and told him I could never see him again. I did not!! I was determined to figure this thing out, but the pain, the insecurities, the loneliness, the failures!!!! I needed validation!!

I did not love me, so it was not hard for anyone to get me to pay attention, and someone did. My husband started calling and looking for me again, and it was not long before we were messing around again, except this time he did not come home like the other times.

I was going to visit him after work and it was going okay, we let go of the past and we would be "friends." Then just like that reality set in, my daughter's court date came up.

We went to court and just like that my daughter was sentenced to six months in jail. I was broken. I still remember standing in the courtroom watching them take my girl away in handcuffs.

My youngest daughter and I left the courthouse a mess! I remember her face as she looked at me as they took her away. I hurt for every mother that has endured or will endure that pain, no matter what the circumstances are. No mother should have to feel that.

That quickly changed the dynamics between us, now I felt guilty! I could not understand how I could be laid up with this man, knowing my daughter was in jail because of something he did. He never had to pick up that phone and dial 911! Yet I was laid up with him. I felt like the bottom of the barrel.

What kind of mother was I? I hated myself even more. My daughter never blamed me at our visits, and I did not miss one. I would leave the Wood at six-thirty in the morning, and I would park at the jail with my alarm on for nine o'clock, the first visit.

My daughter encouraged me to forgive him, to try to fix things. He had to move from the place he was staying and needed somewhere to go. I allowed him to come back home temporarily, that was the deal.

As I was starting to forgive and accept what was, I received a letter in the mail for my husband from the prosecutor's office. I opened it, I sure did. The letter was thanking him for his cooperation on my daughter's prosecution. My heart dropped, I lost it!!!

 I could not believe my eyes!! My daughter was sitting in this disgusting jail and this letter says that he helped! The whole time, I begged him to drop the charges on my daughter and every time he gave me an excuse of why he couldn't that day.

That was the last draw for me. There was no way I was going to be with him after that. During the last seven years I always stayed in contact with the guy from Jersey who broke my heart. He always called. A few months would pass and there he was again.

 Even though we maintained communication, he knew that I was with my husband and that I was trying to make it work, so it never went anywhere.He would remind me that he still loved me and always would! Even though I had heavy trust issues especially with him because of the past, I appreciated that he showed me so much love.

I was a broken woman, who couldn't tell you what it was to love herself even if you paid her, any love was everything!

It was so ironic that I had traveled to Jersey while my husband and I were broken up. While I was there, I didn't even see him and I could've, but I didn't. After reading the letter from the prosecutor I told him he needed to move, that I would give him time to move.

But the more I saw him lying comfortably in my house, thinking about my daughter in that jailhouse my anger grew. I became madder by the second. I was broken, missing my child, and to receive that letter basically told me that he could've dropped the charges.

My child could be here, and we all could be together working on our family, but you chose to hurt her, and hurt me also!

A day or two after the letter, Satan did what he did best he set up my next situation for the perfect mess!!! Jersey as we will call him calls me out of the blue. He was in a program for recovery and wanted to do the usual check in to see how I was doing. I broke down immediately!

I just started crying telling him about the letter and what happened with my baby girl, and he was floored. He was so angry! He just kept asking me "when are you going to learn?"

He reminded me of the past and all the things that I had suffered with my husband, he gave me validation, of course you know I needed that! And just like that I was all in! We started talking every day, all the time. This time he was going to save me!

Yes, this time he would be the one! I make light of the situation because it's the only way I know how to get through life with a joke. I was all gas, no breaks. I was a fool. I forgot about the loving myself part and I did what I always did, I loved someone else.

I thought for seven long years that the reason my marriage probably kept failing was because he wasn't my soulmate. That I needed to find my soulmate, so maybe Jersey was my soul mate. He always validated me, he always told me I was the most beautiful thing on the planet. He wanted me to read him all my writings. He was interested if I wrote anything new.

This was a person who was interested in me. Maybe he was my soulmate and here I was holding myself back from the love that I deserved. I became my mother, even though my husband was still in my house, I got in my car with my daughter and drove to New Jersey.

My intentions were only to go visit him at the rehab, to encourage him, and to show him that I was serious about giving it another chance. I arrived in Trenton a nervous wreck around 3am. I told him that I would see him the next day, but he couldn't wait.

He was taken to the hospital, and I met him there. We were both so nervous after seven years not seeing each other. He was so skinny, was my first thought.

 What happened to him? This wasn't the big guy I knew, I never saw him that way before and it broke me. We sat in the car and talked for an hour or two, then I drove him back to the rehab. He got in trouble for leaving the hospital with me.

They let him stay, but his visit for the next day got cancelled. He was so upset, those two hours had cost us our visit, but not him, anyone who knows him will tell you he had a way with words. He was going to make it happen, and he did. He got us a quick thirty-minute visit, but that wasn't enough for him.

 He was determined to spend time with me since he knew I would be leaving back to Florida soon. He pretended to be sick again and got dropped off at the hospital.

I had two beautiful hotel rooms in West Windsor for my cousin, my daughter, and my nieces and nephews so we could have a small family reunion. We were all by the pool when he called. He asked me to come get him, I did.

We came back to the hotel, and we got in the room and not even five minutes in, he was snoring. He was asleep and he would not move.

 I touched his head, and he was burning up with a fever. I ran to my daughter's room to get a fever reducer and I gave it to him along with antibiotics I had. I let him sleep until the next day. He had to be back a long time ago, and he was willing to lose his spot and be homeless just to spend some time with me and I felt so guilty.

I went into the bathroom while he slept, and I just cried, and cried! I felt cornered! Here I had this man in my house who conspired to have my baby thrown in jail, while this man was fighting an addiction that was killing him, he was homeless, and needed my help. I cried to God, what do I do?

I prayed and cried sitting on the toilet, and out of nowhere I stopped crying. I grabbed my phone and sent my husband a text message, "you have until Tuesday at ten am to find somewhere to go, when I get back from New Jersey please don't be there."

He texts back, "I'll be gone today!" I thanked him, jumped in the shower and cried like a baby. I felt horrible, I was a horrible person! But I was a mother first!

I was disappointed in myself for doing things the way I did, but somehow as I cried in my own shame, I felt a sweet revenge! I reminded myself of the conditions my daughter was living through, the pain I was feeling without her, the pain her sisters were feeling. Also, my mother loves her granddaughters. All my family, we suffered when my daughter walked into that jail!

A mother's pain doesn't ease up, I was in pain all day every day, my daughter is my heart, and I was dying without her.I finished getting dressed and I walked out the bathroom when I noticed he was finally waking up.

It was January and it was snowing outside, so as I looked out the big hotel window something came over me and I knew that I was about to make the right decision. I turned around and I asked him if I could talk to him? He said yes.

I could tell he was still sick; the fever had come back so I gave him more medication, and I started to talk. I asked him would he leave back to Florida with me? He just looked at me and walked away.

He just sat down quietly for what seemed forever. After a while, he told me he had to think about it, this was a big decision. I told him to take his time but just remember I was leaving the next day. He went back to sleep, since he was not feeling good.

While he slept, I drove to pick up his daughter who I had not seen in seven years either. I wanted to surprise him, so I made plans to pick her up, and told him I had to run to the store.

I was so happy to see his daughter, I always felt nothing but love for her and I knew that she had been through so much that it would be nice for her to spend time with her dad. On the way back we talked about her dad leaving with me to Florida, and she was completely on board.

We both knew that this was it, it was time to make a lifesaving choice. Either he would leave, or he would lose his life to drugs and the streets something neither one of us wanted. We finally got back to the hotel, and he was so surprised and happy to see her.

I can still see the happiness in both of their faces, a picture I will always carry. It felt good to do something for someone else and even more seeing how much they appreciated it.

At that moment, the guilt I felt went out the window because I knew that I was helping someone else who needed saving. Just like my mother I had an amazing heart with a knack of making bad decisions.

After a bit of convincing, he agreed and just like that we were on 95 south. I was under the impression that he wanted to change, and I had grand expectations! My youngest daughter supported my decision to bring him back even though she was so hurt that she did not even care anymore.

 She was so happy to be on a road trip and spending some much-needed time with her family that she did not even have time to absorb that just like that, her dad would not be home when we arrived, and I would be starting a new life with a new man.

Chapter 18

We arrived in Florida, and I could see the shock on his face that he was here. For seven years he only wished for this moment, and it was finally here. I was a little upset with him, on the road here, he wanted me to buy him alcohol which was completely contrary to the plan.

I did not let him see I was upset; I was just gonna wait for the right moment to talk to him. Right now, I just wanted him to get comfortable. I wanted to be considerate, I was trying to put myself in his shoes.

I knew he just left the rehab, his family, his friends, and everything he knew. I did not want to put more pressure on him since I know from my own experience that pressure bust pipes. I took him around Vero so he could get familiar with the area. We went to the movies, dinner, and I took him to the beach where he took in every breath of fresh air.

He was so grateful, and I was feeling like I had made the right decision. He was making a habit of getting alcohol on the way home. Again, I was trying to give him a few days.

Now a few days had come and gone, but drinking was still becoming a daily occurrence. It became a problem when I was in the kitchen cooking dinner for us.

My son in law and I were having a deep conversation, and he was even a little emotional since we were talking about the baby my daughter had lost and how it was affecting them. Unfortunately, Jersey had been drinking and I was about to see a side of him I had never seen before. He came into the kitchen where I was cooking and talking and just started going off on me.

He was telling me how I needed to learn when to stop talking, that I talked enough. Mind you I am talking about my daughter's miscarriage, and he is saying that. It threw me through a loop. I could not even understand where this was coming from and why he was acting that way, especially in front of my son in law.

I was so embarrassed, and the more I tried to defuse the conversation, the worst it got. It became an intense argument. At that very moment I wanted out! I could not believe that I had been through so much and I was sitting in my house screaming. Having a shouting match but with a different person.

Same movie, just a different actor. How did I get here?

In the middle of that argument, he told me that he could have any woman he wanted, any time he wanted so I better get my mind right. That struck a nerve, in turn I struck his nose.

I did not see any other women trying to save his life, but still he was under the influence of his biggest vice and was hurting me just like everyone else had. I felt betrayed by him, I felt like after all these years he had never talked to me or treated me the way he was at that moment.

I was dealing with a stranger. He was not the man I thought I knew. After only two weeks, I called and bought him a plane ticket to go back home. I told him I was sorry, but I did not just come out of such a bad place to get into another one.

As much as it hurt me, I did not want to hurt anymore. It was best for him to leave. He was hurt, he regretted drinking and getting out of line with me, and all the drama that had occurred. I accepted his apology, but the ticket was bought, and I was determined to get out before it was too late.

That was all I needed to see, for me to know that I never wanted to be in that situation again. I knew that once we went there, it was going to be easy to come back to this place again! I got a ticket for him for that weekend, and I was in the middle of packing since I was buying my first home amid all that was going on.

I was in the house cleaning with my daughter, and you could cut the air with a knife. It was so thick. He was outside cleaning up when a car pulled up. He was the friendliest person ever, so I was not surprised when five minutes later he was still out there talking.

Fifteen minutes later he was still out there talking, at the time I was so angry and bitter. I was channeling those feelings outward, and I did not care who was getting it. All I knew was time was running out and the property owner was coming to do a final walk through.

We had all been working tirelessly to get it prepared and with just an hour away from her arrival and so many things still to do, why was he out there still chatting? I yelled at him "Are you serious?" He looked back and I yelled out "You know the landlord is about to be here and we have all these things to do, and you out there talking, are you serious?" Sometimes you need to learn how to bite your tongue, because what I did not know was that he was talking to the women of God!

Yes, he was talking about God, and I was worried about all the wrong things. It reminded me of when Jesus went to the house of a woman named Martha, she had a sister called Mary, who sat at the feet of Jesus listening to everything he had to say.

But Martha was distracted by all the preparations that had to be made. Martha, seeing her sister sitting down not helping, went to Jesus and asked him if he did not care that she made her do all the work. She even demanded that he tell Mary to help her!

That's when Jesus said the well-known words found in Luke 10:41-42 "Martha, Martha you are worried and upset about many things, but few things are needed or indeed only one. Mary has chosen what is better, and it will not be taken away from her."

I was convicted. It made me tone down and have one last sit down with him before he left back to Jersey in the next few days. We sat on the porch, and I explained all my feelings, how my past had affected me how his drinking took me to an awfully bad place, including my sexual abuse from childhood since my uncle was an alcoholic.

The smell on his breath reminded me of the smell on my uncle when he was on top of me abusing that little girl. The trauma was still affecting me, and I had to be honest for once.

I was not willing to be with an alcoholic, I could not do it. I apologized because he came all the way here and now, he was going to go back. I told him to look at it as a vacation and that he should go home and change, finish the program. If it were meant to be after he was addiction free, and I had healed from all that was holding me down then, we would revisit this. He agreed.

We were driving to the airport, and he was so upset. He kept telling me to please give him another chance and I just told him I could not. He did not know that I had a way of dealing with life when I was unsure of something. I would give God two choices and whatever happened that would be my sign. I have always done it and I still do.

I had so much faith that I knew nothing was impossible for God and that he would answer me, so I made a deal with him. If he wanted him to leave and go back to New Jersey then he would have no issues with his ID, he would get on the plane and go.

If he did not want him to leave and if he had a purpose for him, and if he wanted me to help him then, he would have an issue with the ID. He would not be allowed on the plane. I was always specific with God and the ID was specific.

I drove and prayed, asking God to decide for me. It was too much for me. I was overwhelmed and I just wanted this to be over already. At the same time there was a big piece of me that did not want him to go. It was as if God had a purpose for him and I had to help him.

As I prayed, I thought about the job that called to offer him an interview right before we left. I did not tell him about it because I did not want to make things worse. The woman who pulled up a few days before, she had invited him to church, and also talked to him about God.

The more I thought about it, the more confused I was feeling. I just yelled out "God please make it clear!" Be careful what you ask for. Immediately the sky turned black, and a storm came down on top of us. I could not see ahead but all the other cars were flying by us. It was so bad I had to pull over and it looked like the rainstorm was only over us.

Noone else was feeling this storm but my car. He looked at me terrified, and I looked back with the same look. He just shook his head and said, "you see God is trying to tell you something but you're hard headed and you won't listen!"

The rain quickly cleared and although he was right, I had made a deal with God, and he would answer me as soon as we got to the airport, so I kept driving until we finally arrived.

I parked my car in the parking garage, and we walked to the Orlando airport to check in.

We checked in and they asked for his ID, the lady looked at it, gave it back, gave him his ticket and told him to walk around to the security checkpoint to board the flight. I got my answer. It was clear there were no issues with the ID and God wanted him to go. I had recently seen my God's hand, not even a week before my house closing.

The IRS took my entire eight thousand dollars tax refund for my school loans. That was my money to close on my house and with a week away from closing how could I produce four thousand dollars? BUT GOD!!!!!!!!

I remember the morning I got the notification. It was about three in the morning time for the morning run, when the IRS sent me the notice. I ran out of the hospital with my best friend following me in a bath of tears. What would I do? I was so anxious but there was nothing I could do but make the call to cancel my closing!

With a broken heart and an embarrassed face, I called my property owner who was also my realtor. The same one who took a chance on me two years ago and rented me the amazing house only God could give me.

I told her everything that happened as I swallowed my tears. She told me to give her a minute and she would call me back. Within an hour she called me back, she had called and found out the exact amount we needed for closing and told me she had a solution for me. I was able to borrow more than what I needed so that I could have money to move and be okay.

I praised God and thanked her! My faith grew stronger than the last miracle he performed. My faith was at an all-time high! I knew that God wanted him to leave because they accepted his ID so now, I could tell him about my deal with God!

As we got to the security checkpoint, he looked at me and begged me not to do this! Not to send him home, and then I told him about the deal. I told him God had chosen, and I had to obey God. I was so sorry, but he had to go. We hugged and he walked away with tears in his eyes.

I stood there watching as he walked away, and my tears just fell. I was hurting and I looked down when I realized he left the book I gave him. I started running around the checkpoints to get to the other side so I could give him his book. I also wanted to give him another hug because I felt so bad. I finally got to him, and I just grabbed him, turned him around and hugged him.

He was shocked, he did not know where I came from, but he was looking overwhelmed like he saw a ghost. I asked him what was wrong? At that moment he would see how important obedience and faith were!

He looked at me with this shocking look on his face and said to me "They won't let me in, they said my ID won't work!" I just jumped up and down, grabbed him over that black divider and just screamed all through the airport as I hugged him!

God had spoken and I would help him!! We hugged for what felt like forever in the airport and then again when we got to the car. It was as if we both got scared straight, and we knew that we had to change. We sat in the car, and he was so shocked about the ID.

He could not even talk, he kept saying, "you told me that you made a deal with God specifically with the ID, I wasn't let in because of the ID!" I was not as shocked as him because the God that I serve had been showing me miracles and signs my whole life so all it did was make my faith stronger!

As we drove back and the face of shock still very apparent in his face, I figured I would blow his mind more. I gave him the big news that not only was he able to stay, but God also set up an interview for him. He was floored!

After seeing God so clear he was determined to change his life and I was determined to help him! Immediately I reached out to the lady who pulled up and apologized for my ignorance and that I was so ashamed.

We met up with her and she hugged us both, we gave her the airport testimony and she took us in as her daughter and her son.

I am so blessed to say that mom is still in my life today. We rented a U-Haul and just like that we moved into my first home. I was now a homeowner, and I could not be more thrilled! We decided right from the beginning that we were going to put God first and that we were going to go to church.

I was so embarrassed, but with all the shame I still mustered up the courage to go back to my home church. How could I show up to church with this new guy, when I was still a married woman? I expressed my feelings to him, but he convinced me that we were going for God and with an expectation. I had to put my head up and focus on the King!

We arrived at church, and we sat on the far right. At first, I just wanted to dig a hole and get in it, but thankfully my best friend came with her daughter to support us. We sat listening as the pastor preached the word and I do not think I got most of it. I was so wrapped up in my own shame. Then just like that the pastor asked if anyone had a testimony and before I could say stop, Jersey was halfway up to the mic, and I felt myself sinking in the chair.

 God, please help me, I thought to myself! He diddy bopped all the way to the stage, that is what I called his walk. Bravely he picked up that mic and in front of the church he testified about a woman who saved an addict like him, and the love of God who stopped him from getting on that flight so he could be there testifying on that day. He finished off telling everyone in the church that I was his woman and that we would be around much more so get used to us! The church went crazy! He had that effect on people! We both did and that is why we connected!

He started working and you could see his look changing, you could see the glow of God in him.He was getting bigger and bigger, he was finally the man I knew. I was so proud to see all his arduous work. We enjoyed reading the bible together, and Christian books. We were growing and finally at peace.

He made the decision that he wanted to get saved, so he was baptized at St Matthew's Missionary Church in the same pool, my daughter and I had dedicated our lives to Christ in.

We were active in church, and we started talking about me getting a divorce so we could get married at the church and live our lives the way Christ intended us to live. We were happy! I warned him before he got baptized to be prepared to face Satan's raft and that he would begin to experience trials and tribulations.

He looked at me like I was crazy, but I had been in the spiritual realm so long I already knew what was next. It was not that I was expecting something bad, I just wanted to be prepared for anything the enemy would bring. He was very tactful and once we got comfortable, he would move.

I could see us getting comfortable, so I was staying busier in my word. One day just like that he came home from work and there it was the can of beer that would be the beginning of a tragic end. I did not think too much about it at first, I knew that he worked hard at the carwash all day and he had a bad hip that prevented him from doing much of anything without pain, so I was okay with it. Then it started becoming a daily thing again, and soon he was not doing the things he was doing before.

Our bible reading depleted and just like that our church attendance did too. I was trying so hard to get through to him but now that he was getting drunk again, it would turn into an argument and the last thing I needed was that.

I was still coping with my daughter being in jail and three months of visits, work, and the everyday hustle was getting to me but still I was holding on to faith! You can see my thought process in this journal entry I wrote on March 20, 2019:

"Can't believe it's been almost three years since I wrote in this journal. Here I am once again!!! Saying the same thing... So much has changed! Not only do I have one granddaughter but now we have a second queen!

I am the proud grandmother of two beautiful little girls that I can't get enough of! They are my everything! My oldest moved into her own castle with the father of her girls and they continue to work together to give my babies a great life. Not a perfect life but a blessed one!

My baby girl has been sitting in jail since December 17, 2018, and that has taken a toll on me. The circumstances that led her there are very painful especially when the man I trusted to raise my daughters is the reason behind her incarceration!

It is a very painful process that I believe God will use for our good. That man is no longer in our lives and has no power to cause any more pain to my children or myself. For that I am grateful.

My youngest is still battling the pain that comes from abandonment and the loss of her first child. I believe her healing is also on the way! She is learning to forgive, to love, to heal, and I am sure that God will turn all those pains into strength!

She is a strong beautiful woman. I cannot even imagine what the future holds for her! As for me I am also learning to heal, to trust, and to love. I never knew how hard it could be. I have been in such hard places in my life that today as I sit in a softer place, it is harder to adjust when I am so used to a concrete floor. If you are not used to sleeping in a soft bed it can be painful.

I purchased my first home this month! I am now a homeowner! Crazy but true! I'm so blessed! I am so grateful that God has given me a little corner to call my own, that my children and grandchildren can call their own! It is something I always wanted and now as I sit here, I am so grateful that God thinks so much of me!

I pray every day for self-healing, physical-healing, mental-healing, and spiritual-healing. Every day I see change today I make forty-eight hours without smoking and I feel clear minded, I am in awe with God. How quick he can remove the desire out of your body if that is truly what you want. You just have to want it!

I sit here and I enjoy this day off rocking on my porch looking at the sky and as I speak to God, I just can't wait to see what all he has planned for me. Who will I become? When will I heal? When will I be able to love freely and the right way?

When will I be free from these walls that I have built for so long! A prison! I put them there to protect me, now they have become a part of me. Every time I am ready to take down one brick, I feel like I get hurt somehow. Even if the wrong thing is said to me, especially in an aggressive way I grab a slab of concrete and put that brick right back.

I'm just not willing to be hurt, especially by words. Those are the worst things for me. Maybe because people have always used words. Anger, yelling, and screaming to hurt me. I do not know, but I know this place I am in is foreign. I am not sure how I feel about it. I know I am at a place in my life where I need pure peace, true happiness, and the freedom to love. I honestly can say I am not there yet.

This man I am with makes it so hard, we had a bad fight, and he mentioned my past, something I would never imagine him to do. I trusted him with my secrets, and he used them all against me in a fight. He brought a person out that I hate, the anger and the betrayal made me black out and I grabbed a glass and threw it at his head. I thank God for grace and speed because he ducked, and it broke right through the window. I cannot continue in this place of destruction; I cannot continue to allow other people to break my spirit like this!

I am full of insecurities that were dug into me, from others' own insecurities about me. But I know I need to change, and I know I need to start somewhere, it's my relationship with God for me! I know I can trust God; I cannot lose with God! I know God will never leave me or forsake me. So here I sit, with a new understanding. If I can just master my relationship with God then all things will be worked out for my good, at the right time, in God's perfect timing and his perfect way!

So today I am letting go and letting God! He is the author and editor of my book. If I let him stay in control, all things will work out no matter what the end results! It feels so good to allow GOD to work without getting in his way! He needs no help from me!"

Chapter 19

I started to focus more on God and less on the pain I was feeling from the betrayal. I started focusing on forgiveness and getting things ready because soon my daughter would be coming home. I didn't want her to come home to a hostile environment.

My youngest daughter and her boyfriend were living with us and had to deal with the yelling and the screaming which was bad enough. My youngest and I talked, and I knew things had to change. I didn't want to cause my daughter more damage when she came home.

The day was finally here, my daughter would be released late at night, so Jersey went with me to go pick her up. I was so anxious waiting for my baby, it had been a long five months apart with only seeing her through a video call. I needed to hug my girl and kiss her!

The hours passed and still no sign of my daughter. I just wanted her to come out. He told me how happy he was for me. We talked for a little bit about all I had suffered to get there today and that hopefully this would bring peace to our home. After what seemed forever, out of nowhere I saw my baby coming out! I just remember us both taking off running at the same time!!!

It was a scene from a love movie, there wasn't a dry eye in the room. That reunion even brought Jersey to tears. We stood there screaming, hugging, kissing, and telling each other how much we missed each other as we cried full of relief that finally this nightmare would be over.

I was wrong, I didn't know the effect jail would have on my girl, I thought she would come home one way, but she came home angry. I remember a close friend warning me this would happen, but I didn't listen. She was isolated in her room, that I had dolled up for her. I would go in and spend time with her and watch movies, just excited to be able to do that after so long.

The conversations were always the same, "Mami, I'm a felon now! My career is ruined, what am I supposed to do with my life now?" as the tears poured down our cheeks. We both knew how hard she had worked to become a CNA, with future goals of going to college and growing in the medical field. I tried so hard to comfort her but there were really no words that I could find that would change her situation. All I could say was the most importanthing I could tell her "TRUST GOD!"

Things were hard for a while as she adjusted to being home, but we managed, and we continued to move forward. I was still working at Lawnwood, and I was focused on getting my life in order. About five months passed and Jersey was still battling the alcohol, but because I was working overnight it wasn't affecting us. He learned to drink when I wasn't around, and I learned to ignore all the empty bottles of E&J I found in his drawers. I was tired, and at that point nothing had happened so I thought things would be okay. My cousin and his wife were having a big birthday party for their two daughters, and they invited us to go to Tampa.

At first, I was going to go alone, and take my daughters. For some odd reason, I had a bad feeling about inviting him to go with us. When I mentioned it to him, he got really upset that I would even go without him. I talked to my cousin's wife who I consider my sister, and she told me it was fine.

She rented two hotel rooms for my daughters and us to stay comfortably and told us everything was set for our trip. I was so excited about finally introducing her to this guy I talked so highly about. In my mind I kept playing out our first vacation, how we would dance in the middle of the dance floor, like we did almost eight years ago.

We used to take over the dance floor at Champ's. You could see the connection from across the room, I was looking forward to feeling their vibes again! Maybe this was all we needed to rekindle our love. I could not wait! Finally, the time had come. It was August and it was time to get on the road and head to Tampa, but before we left, I wanted to have a talk with Jersey. I sat him down and told him how important this was for me!

I was finally going to have the opportunity to bring him around my family! I explained that I didn't want to be embarrassed so please just for these two days not drink at all. He agreed. We got in the car and off we were. We stopped at the gas station to get gas before we got on the road, and he went into the store. Never could I imagine that after we just had that conversation, ten minutes later he would come out with a beer in his hand. He did!

I was so upset because if he would have asked me not to do something, without a doubt I would've done it. He was big on respect, yet now he had none for my daughters, my family, or I. We both knew where his drinking would lead. I have had enough experience to know. I wasn't talking the whole ride and I just focused on the road. We arrived and I shook it off. It was just a beer, and he was going to act right, so I had no reason to be mad. Who was I fooling?

Immediately after we arrived in the room, my cousin came over. She had flown in from New Jersey and was waiting to see me. As soon as I introduced him to my cousin his first words after "nice to meet you" were "Where's the drinks?" I couldn't believe him. But again, I didn't want to ruin the moment, so I went with my cousin to her room to get the liquor she had. I said to myself "We're going to have one drink together with my cousin and everything will be fine."

We got back to the room and my cousin said she had Crown Royal Apple or some Wine? He said he was going to have both. I thought of the beer he drank and now these two completely opposite drinks, I was in big trouble!

I knew him well enough to know that nothing good was going to come out of that night and it didn't!

My cousin headed out to the venue, and she told me that she would meet me there. I had to get ready. I arrived late. Jersey started acting weird immediately, without saying a word to me he went outside which was not like him.

His not drinking self, would be worrying about what I was wearing and what I was putting with what! He was a very attentive man, he was a wonderful man, but the alcohol destroyed all the beauty for me, and I could not see any of it after that.

I finished getting ready and I thought well he just wants to see me all dressed up! He is going to be so happy when he sees me, and I was wrong. He was out there talking to some strangers which was not surprising at all. That was his personality, but never ignored me. That was not like him at all.

He was the type of person that worshipped the ground I walked on. But once he got that alcohol in his system, he was a completely different person. There was no trace of the person I was trying to learn how to love again. After what he had said to me, I was deeply wounded!

I opened the car door and I sat in the car waiting for my daughters, and him to get in the car. I just prayed that I would not be embarrassed, but I must have not prayed hard enough. That night he completely embarrassed me. He began to drink immediately after we arrived at the party. I went and served him a big plate of food so that he could eat and absorb all that alcohol.

He told me to set it on the table and he just continued to drink. He was getting drunker by the minute, and it was still light outside. My cousin grabbed me and took me to see all the party favors, and the cake. We were so excited to be together, it had been so long. It was supposed to be a memorable celebration. I knew how far they had come to get here. All the struggle and sacrifice to have this Sweet Sixteen. Instead, it would only be remembered by the night my man acted a fool in front of all my family. I would be stuck apologizing for days to come.

After arguing with other guests at the party, he started talking badly about the performer. He was doing drag, and what he did not know was that he was the father of my cousin's best friend and he made disturbing comments in front of her. Twice I was pulled aside to be told to get him. I finally convinced him to eat, and he did. After eating I prayed, he would relax before we got to a point of no return, but I had no idea we already were at that point.

 Not long after he ate, I got pulled aside again. This time he was disrespecting my niece and my daughter, I was about to blow a gasket! Why was he doing this to me? I had been nothing but good to him, we had been serving God everything was going so well, how could we be here, I could not understand. I went out and had a talk with him for the third time begging him to stop and he was getting louder and louder to the point my family came out to see what was going on. I was so embarrassed, but still I was trying to save face. He finally sat down outside where everyone was smoking and not long after I was pulled aside again. He was sleeping outside on the chair.

I could not take one more embarrassment so I told my kids and my cousins that I would be back, and I woke him up. I told him it was time to leave. We got in the car, and he asked where my girls were? I told him that I was going to come back and pick them up when they were ready, and he lost it. He began punching the windshield and trying to jump out the car on the highway and police were on the side of us. I was trying to drive and trying to grab him at the same time.

How could I be in this toxic situation once again, when God knows all I wanted was peace, love, and happiness. I was so nervous; I had never seen him this way. He began calling me every name in the book except holy. I was devastated but I was honestly so scared in that car that I did not dare to say a word. We arrived at the hotel, and he jumped out of the car. I just pulled off. I did not care if he got in the room or what he did. All I knew was that for my own mental health and my own safety I needed to go and I needed to go immediately.

I got back to the party, and finally I was having a fun time. My cousins were all dancing with my kids, and they were so happy I was back. We danced one song, and that quick, it was done. I got pulled aside again. What now? My cousin said that he was making a huge scene at the hotel and that the manager called to complain.

I could not believe this was happening, so I called the manager back and apologized and asked him to just please give him a key to the room so he could sleep it off. We arrived shortly back to the hotel, and he was already asleep. I was so grateful because I could not endure another second if he were still up fighting. God heard my prayers I thought as I quietly climbed in bed and slept at the edge.

I did not want to be nowhere near him. I knew I could not come back from this. Nine months and I was calling it quits. The next morning all the family met in the cafeteria for breakfast, and he stood outside talking to strangers the whole time. I was waiting thinking only if he comes and apologizes to my family. Only if he would show face, but he did not. At that point it was confirmation that I could never face my family again if I stayed in this toxic relationship.

We arrived back in Vero. I was so ashamed, I apologized repeatedly, but I could tell my family was hurt and more for me. They had watched me go through so much and they were rooting for us. I had spoken so highly of him before I went to Tampa. I could not believe he made me look like such a fool. As soon as we got home, I gathered some things, and I went to stay in my daughter's room.

I told him to stop paying bills and start saving all his money because I needed him to find his own place. I was not going to rush him to leave, but he needed to start preparing for his future. He apologized and begged me to fix things, but it was too late for me. I was trying to heal from the last fight that left me feeling scared about how terrible things could really get.

I could not and I just was not going to. My daughters told me how embarrassed they were, my cousin expressed her disappointment in him. She had a long talk with me. Telling me how I deserve so much more than that, and after seeing me hurt for so many years, it hurt her to see that I was still in this vicious circle. I agreed.

I could not do this; it was time to let go. Things were brought to a halt when we were hit with a hurricane. His move would have to wait. I was locked in at the hospital for the hurricane, and we had to come together to board the house. After me screaming and yelling, he and my nephew finally figured it out.

I was happy that at least I could go stay a few days at the hospital and get away from the stress that was at home. I didn't even want to be there. We had a blast at the hospital, after so many years working together, it felt like a family sleepover.

We were having dinner in the break room, watching the news when I got an unexpected message from my ex-girlfriend. The one from seventeen years before. The one I almost ran over on her motorcycle. I was excited to hear from her, but shocked as well. After watching the news, she wanted to make sure I was okay. I thanked her for reaching out and smiled.

When the hurricane was over, and I arrived at home I tried to be cordial. I was grateful for him boarding the house. I was appreciative, and he knew it. September came and he was supposed to be saving his money for his spot. I was still staying in my daughter's room. I was at work one night and I was telling my best friend how bad my birthday was the year before, how I had two pink eyes and could not do anything at all. I decided I wanted to do a makeup birthday, so we would have a pre-birthday bash for me the first week of September and then a birthday party for my actual birthday at the end of the month.

Even though things were over between us I still let him know that I was going out that night with my best friends and that my daughter would also be going also. I did not want him to get the wrong impression and act out. I still remembered the fear I had felt a few weeks before.

I met up with my friends. My daughter met us at the square grouper in Fort Pierce, FL. It is a warm restaurant on the intercoastal, and you can enjoy sitting at the tiki bar by having drinks by the water. I needed this girl time. It had been so long since I had been out with my friends. I was so excited to have some catch up time and just hang out.

We stayed there until one and then my friend said, "I know you didn't make me get dressed up for your birthday bash to go home this early!" I already knew what that meant! We were heading down south, that is our thing! We jumped in the car and headed to West Palm Beach to enjoy the rest of the night.

We ended up getting back to Vero at 7:30 am. We bar hopped all night and then we went out for Colombian hot dogs and fries! That is how we always did. We drank, danced, ate, and went home happy. It has been our tradition for over ten years. I arrived at home, and since I knew I arrived so late and knowing the type of man I was dealing with, I went right to our room to avoid any problems.

I figured if I got in the bed with him, he would not question me, I was sure I smelled of alcohol, cigarettes, and hot dogs. I was feeling so nice, and I no more than hit the pillow I was snoring. He left for work, and when he came back, I was still sleeping. I had such a hangover; I could not get up.

He was so upset with me, and I could feel the energy in the air. So, I got up and went to the sofa where I passed out again. I was suddenly awakened by his screams and yells and name calling. He did it again, he went out, got drunk, came back, and lost it. My nightmare had just become a reality again. I was so hung over; I had no energy to fight. I just let him scream obscenities at me.

He then started demanding that I give him money, I was so confused. He was supposed to be saving his money all this time. Now I was even more concerned! I got my purse, and I went and sat on the porch trying to avoid any problems, but that did not work. He stood at the door going off about me not coming home and acting crazy. Then he started to make insane accusations, he accused me of sleeping with my daughter's boyfriend and of having a threesome with my daughter!

I knew alcohol changed him, but he had gone too far! This was worse than Tampa and I was so tired! I didn't even respond to him because I did not have the energy until he struck a chord. He told me that after he left wherever he saw me he was going to put hands on me. That was it for me, one thing about me I never took threats lightly.

 I stood up with my purse in my arm and told him to do it, because I was right there and there was no reason to wait. He jumped at me to make me jump, but instead my reflex reacted, and I hit the glass dish he had in his hand. When I hit the plate up, it hit him between the eyes, and I just saw the blood gushing out.

I was so scared; this is exactly what I was afraid of. Someone getting hurt. I knew I had beat a case in the past when I was facing twenty years in prison, there was no way that I was going to go through that again.

My daughter finally came and tried tirelessly to get him to go to the hospital. There was blood everywhere all through the house. It looked like someone was murdered there. I was having flashbacks and PTSD so bad. I just wanted to go. Finally, after a long time convincing him, he went to the hospital. Seven stitches. He came back home, and I did not say anything at all.

I already felt bad that it happened, but I could not talk to him. I stayed in my daughter's room in a nervous state because I was trying so hard to avoid all of this and here we were again. I sent him a message and told him he could stay until his payday and that day he would have to get a ticket and go back to Jersey.

It was not healthy or safe for him to stay with me any longer. He was upset but he agreed. I left it alone and waited patiently until the day came. Payday came and he had all his things packed. Just the way he came, he left. When he left, I assumed he was being dropped off at the airport, or bus station. I never expected what happened next.

 He did not leave, instead he chose to stay in Vero and get a hotel. That is what he told me he was doing. I told him that I felt bad he was there since I brought him out here, but the things he had done had caused me to fear that it would get worse if we did not end it then.

For a while he called me every night like clockwork while I was at work, but he never called to talk. It was always a fight and being nasty to each other. I was not going to do that any longer, so I stopped answering and I chose that the best thing for me was to move on and that is what I did. Months would pass before I would hear from him again, but for now I was determined to finally learn to love myself.

Chapter 20

I was finally getting used to the single life. Some weeks had passed, and I was doing just fine. I was glad to hear that Jersey had found someone else here in Vero and that he had even gotten married. I was hurt, but I knew him. He was a survivalist, and to survive he would do whatever it took. So, I didn't allow myself to take it too personally, even though inside I knew I did.

I knew it was done and it was over. I was also over men, and I told myself I would never be with another man and allow him to do me this way again. So alone I would stay, or would I?

I was sitting down in the lab talking to my sis/best friend as we normally do every night on our shifts together. I was fast at drawing, so my floor would be cleaned, and I would have time to help her process. As we processed and got that work done, we would have a blast keeping each other strong through hard times.

I was telling her how even though Jersey had moved on, I was so proud of myself because I was still alone and keeping myself strong and focused on loving myself. Then out of nowhere I get a notification on my messenger. It was a message that was about to change my life once again.

It was my ex-girlfriend. She had checked in on me when the hurricane hit. It was nothing more than a quick hi and bye and yes, I am safe. I didn't think anything of it when I saw the message. I figured she was just saying hi and checking in on me. I was glad that she thought about me, my phone was so dry I thought it was going to turn into dust.

The conversation that started as a hey continued all through the morning and it continued the next day. We talked like we never stopped talking. We took endless selfies, and sent each other pictures all day, or we would video chat. The conversations kept going day after day and they got deeper each day that passed by.

We started reliving the past and I even apologized for hurting her back then. She confessed to me how badly that had affected her life and all the trouble she got into after I broke her heart. At that moment I decided that I was going to make up for my mistakes. I would be a blessing this time, and I wouldn't take her friendship for granted. She was such a good person and she had never done anything but good. Not only for me but my daughters also. Even though it was seventeen years I still appreciated it.

I was starting to feel good again, I was getting my glow back. I was taking care of myself again, taking the time out to care for me, something I had a habit of not doing when I was with these men. My energy was back! My husband once said that I only looked good when I was single, maybe he was right, but maybe it was the way they made me feel that would make me feel insecure about myself.

Maybe it was the insecurities and jealousy that they would radiate towards me. Either way I was glad to be putting effort into looking and feeling my best, I deserved it. We decided to give it a go, we wanted to try again. We believed that we could make each other happy and forget about all the bad things we both had endured in the seventeen years we had been separated.

 Just like that, we started planning a reunion. We talked on the phone all day, even to the point that we were falling asleep on the phone, and it was nice to have someone there. Not physically there because I still wanted to learn how to love myself, and this time I refused to move in with someone when I knew I was far from healed.

 Things were going great at work, I had amazing coworkers and we were more like family. I was loving my grandbabies every chance I got! That was my favorite part of life, and it still is besides God! I was spending time video chatting with my best friend who had lost his mother and needed me more now than ever! I was grateful that I was finally in a place in my life where I could be there for him! I hurt him many times because of my first and second husband.

They both had jealousy issues when it came to our friendship. They could not believe that a man and woman could be only best friends, but they were both wrong. I was even more wrong than both, because I knew that we were only best friends. We have only been best friends since we were twelve years old, and I allowed other people to tarnish our friendship! All because of their own insecurities and their own feelings. I was glad that my best friend was still there after all these years and that we were still like twelve-year-old kids.

Listening to music, playing with filters, and eating on camera. Wish we had messengers when we were growing up! We still do this even now. I love my brother from another mother.

October 19, 2019, my daughter got married. I was blessed to help her get dressed, and even put on her veil. She looked stunning! My baby girl was married!! I was full of joy; her happiness is my happiness! I was happy that my mother came for her wedding, and although she wasn't talking to me, she was cordial. If I could be around her and see her that was sufficient. I was so happy, only if she knew how much I loved her I thought, as I watched her from across the room.

 My heart was full, I was surrounded by the people I love the most! I was finally feeling peace, I was in a good place, and it showed! In only ten days I would be reuniting with my girlfriend after seventeen years. I was so nervous but so excited at the same time.

I was also feeling a little anxious because before I started talking to her, I got word that my husband had gotten arrested and was sentenced to eleven months in prison. As bad as I wanted to not care, I still cared. I contacted him in prison and immediately I decided that I was going to be there for him. If I was there for him, then we could finally find forgiveness and build a friendship.

I knew he didn't have anyone else, so I chose to be there. I was glad I did. Something that would one day come back to haunt me. We kept the conversations cordial and we spoke about moving forward and letting go of the past. It was crazy because my daughter pushed me to help him, even though he didn't reach out to her not once in the five months when she was in jail. No contact whatsoever. My daughter has her mother's heart. Just like me all she knows is forgiveness. I would question myself repeatedly but no matter what, I felt that I was doing what I would want him to do for me.

The exact thing Jesus would do if he was in the same situation. So, I forgave and kept supporting him in his time of need. Especially, when you never know when you may need someone no matter what the past looked like.

Almost a year had passed since I saw him so there was no reason to keep holding on to the past. At the same time Jersey contacted me as well, he asked me to come meet him. I agreed, only because I was determined to have peace. I didn't want to be angry with anyone or hold grudges. I was starting a new relationship with a woman, and I would have to face my own challenges with my family for coming out.

Being angry with him was not something I needed in my life. I picked him up and we went out to the beach. He showed me his wedding band, and I congratulated him. I told him I was sincerely happy for him. I told him I only wanted the best for him, his happiness was all that I wanted. We were both in need of that long conversation.

He apologized to me for everything and thanked me for all that I did. He had realized that although he had some hard days when he left my house, that he knew that I showed him a different life. He was so grateful for his life and how far he had come. He never gave up no matter what! He was so proud that he didn't go back to Jersey, and even though it was tough for him, he said it was always better to be homeless by the beach than in Jersey any day.

That was a story we both knew well. I myself knew homelessness. I had been there myself more than once. Sadly, I was a woman with three kids. Just the other day my daughter called me to tell me, she was so grateful for me. I was taken by surprise, that's not something she does.

I asked her why? That's when she reminded me of how every time, we were homeless, on the run, or in the worst situations I always made it fun! She told me that they never knew how hard things were for me, how stressed I truly was under what I showed them. Now that she is on her own and it is her turn to take the world by the horns, she understands how hard this life really is.

That really did something for me. I needed that boost. Some days are easier than others, but I would be a liar if I don't tell you that, many days

I just want to give up. I get so scared to publish this book, to let you into my world, and let you see the true me! That's when I know I am doing the right thing.

This life is not for the weak. Life is for those that go harder every single time they fall. They know it hurts, it is embarrassing, but it is necessary to build character, to build strength, and integrity. Jersey and I had one important thing in common, and that was we NEVER GIVE UP!!!!

I can still remember how he exercised every day. The pushups on the bathtub. He always said that exercise wasn't only for the body but also for the mind. Now I exercise every day, and I am thankful for that lesson. I understand now, I get it. We must push hard! Never stop moving forward! Forgiveness is part of that. For self, and for others.

I apologized for having to have him leave but I had to do what was right for me and my kids. He agreed, he told me he didn't blame me, that he knew that my intentions for him were always good. He knew I just wanted the best for him, I wanted him to be healthy and get back right with God. When he left me, he realized what was done, and started making positive changes. I was proud of him.

He knew I was dating the girl and we laughed, he said she was so cute to him. He loved her swagg and it was great to be laughing again like the good old days. We listened to some of our favorite songs, and promised to do it again in the future. We started off as friends there was no reason not to be friends. I was so grateful, I was healing, and all those that I loved even if things didn't work out, we were in a good space.

Even the father of my children and I were finally at peace. No grudges, no hard feelings, no bad blood. We were at peace. He lost so many loved ones, and so many years have passed. Why should our grandchildren have to live through any of that toxicity we took our children through? We both understood that now. Finally, with all that out of the way, I was ready for our big reunion. After a long month on the phone, she finally arrived at Orlando airport. We nervously gave each other a quick kiss on the cheek. I could tell she was freaking out. I was too!

My daughter came with me to pick her up and I was just praying that this would work out, I just wanted to be happy. My daughter had to do something while we were in Orlando, so I thought it was a good opportunity for her and me to go somewhere and have a cocktail and catch up. We got dropped off and I could tell she was uncomfortable. She looked nervous, so I quickly grabbed us a drink and we sat at an outdoor table.

I started making conversation to try to calm her down. It was seventeen years, and deep inside I was super nervous too. Finally, my daughter came back, and we drove back to Vero. She started loosening up and I caught a glimpse of the girl that I remembered.

Our relationship grew quickly after that, once we got back to my house it was natural. We were both highly organized and we did so many things alike that it was easy with us. We spent time together and got some rest, we had a busy week ahead before she headed back home again.

We enjoyed the local beaches and drove up and down South Florida. We partied the whole week, we ate amazing food, and even met with her mom in Orlando. We went to Disney and for the first time in a long time, I was happy! I was on roller coasters facing my fear of heights and I felt alive again! I was fifteen the last time I felt like this, it was on a field trip to Great Adventure. I still remember how amazing it felt to be around a loving family. Her mom took me in and immediately was so loving and kind. I was in the most foreign place I had ever been, and I was so grateful that I was smiling again. I was not thinking about anything negative, just enjoying the avatar ride in Animal Kingdom feeling on top of the world.

The week ended and it was time for her to go back home. I was sad to see her leave, but I was okay. I was already used to living alone. I enjoyed it. I was loving myself for once. I was working, going out with my friends, and I was okay with not having someone around all the time. My favorite part was that for the first time in my life, I was with someone who trusted me! She never questions me about anything, and I love that!

It made me want to be more loyal to her, the long distance did not matter to me at all! I was enjoying every minute of life! I loved work, loved being a grandma, life was good. Thanksgiving came, I was working, and she spent her holidays with her family. I was so thankful for my best friend. I had not cooked, and she brought me a big plate with all the fixings.

 I was so grateful for her. I was sad I was not with my daughters and granddaughters. I always cooked huge Thanksgiving Dinners, and we always celebrated together. It was our favorite holiday and there I sat in the lab thinking about my babies. There was nothing a day off and partying with my friends could not fix..... so partied we did.

 My girlfriend and I already had her next trip planned. She would come down for Christmas. Then just like that, things changed. I got a call that my father's wife was in the hospital and needed emergency surgery. I was on a plane back home to Jersey. No matter what had happened in the past, things had changed.

We all have grown through many lessons, and we know how important family is. Life has taught us that none of us is free of sin, and when you are standing pointing one finger there are four pointing back at you. I love my cousin so much and I just wanted to be there for her and my siblings in this time of need. Nothing else mattered except that we were together and that my cousin was okay.

After many prayers, thankfully she was on the road to recovery! I was so glad! I remember in 2016 when I went to Puerto Rico, she was in so much pain and I still remember how hurt I felt seeing her that way. So many moments when I needed her, she was there for me, it was so good to be able to be there too.

It was a treat for my girlfriend and I, this gave me the chance to visit her for the first time. We took full advantage and spent the time I was there with our families. I met hers, she met mine, I was surprised how fast we were moving. I was enjoying every moment. Her mom surprised us with our Christmas gifts while I was there, she got me the cutest MK purse, I never had anyone do anything like that for me, I was blown away.

I was not used to gifts, I was never really given anything, it was rare, most of my gifts came from my daughters. This was new, but I was loving it so much! I was so proud of my relationship with her, I felt free. It was time to go back home, I got a ticket on the same flight with my girlfriend, she was coming to Florida for the holidays. Just like that we were flying together for the first time, something I never did with anyone I was ever with.

In such a brief time I had experienced so many new things with her and I could not wait to share a lifetime with her! We arrived in Florida, where we had gotten a resort in Orlando. We were excited to have an enjoyable time. My daughter came up to meet with us. As I look back, that would be the last time I would see that amazing, pure smile on my girlfriend's face. It would be a long time before I would see her smile again.

We decided to go to Wal-Mart and to the local Spanish grocery store to get groceries so we could cook dinner. That is when she got a phone call that would change our lives forever. Her best friend lost her life in a tragic car accident. If I could go back now that I know how important of a part she played in her life, I would have reacted a lot differently. I was compassionate but now that I know, I would have pulled the car over, grabbed her, hugged her, and let her cry it out. I held her hand as the tears ran down her face, my heart hurt so much for her, and for her best friend's family, such a young beautiful soul gone too soon.

I tried to comfort her with God's promise that we will see our loved ones again. I knew that was the only thing that had gotten me where I was today. I continue to hold on to that faith. We never get over the loss of a loved one, we just keep them alive until their return. She was broken, but she still tried to get through our planned vacation. Forcing smiles in pictures when I knew she was dying inside.

Everywhere we went she was reminded of her best friend who loved Mickey Mouse. Here in the middle of Disney all she could do was think of her best friend, her ride or die. Every moment was getting harder and harder for her.

We went back to Vero and that is when she started to shut down and it was extremely hard for me to be there for her. We got back to my house, and I knew she was going through it. She was here when she should be back home in Amboy for her best friend's funeral. She was not able to make it. I knew that she felt terrible, so I just tried to give her space.

It was Christmas Eve, and we ended up in our first argument and we just went to sleep. I appreciated the fact that it was not out of hand and that it was not anything that got out of control. Compared to my past toxic relationships, that was easy. I happily fell asleep and the next morning we opened gifts and moved on. Finally, someone who does not sit around holding grudges forever. Someone willing to say I am sorry when she is wrong. A best friend who, even though, was living one of her worst moments, still put on matching Christmas pajamas and smiled when she really wanted to scream! It was time for her to go and just like that she was gone. My heart hurt. Still, I continued working, focusing on everyday life. I was trying to support my girlfriend facing this huge loss.

Immediately we started planning her next trip back! My best friend's birthday party was in January, and it would be something that could cheer her up. It would be EPIC!!!! My girlfriend and I were only together for four months but already we had so many things we were doing together, including selling eyelashes and sunglasses.

 Together we were a power couple, we motivated each other, and we made moves together, for the first time I was part of a team. I was so used to always being in competition with these men, and finally someone who wanted to grow with me instead of against me. We took advantage and went on a small cruise with my daughter before the big birthday bash that I would host! I was the hostess with the mostess!

 So much that my girlfriend and I would end up in jail that night. My daughter had to come bail us out, and my selfish actions once again would affect someone other than just me. I was sleeping like a baby in the cell, while my daughter sat there all-night waiting for me to get out. I was being selfish, and I was only thinking about myself.

I was partying and living my best life. That is what I was telling myself. The truth was that when the alcohol hit, underneath all those smiles was a very damaged person. We continued to go back and forth during the next few months. We enjoyed Valentine's in Manhattan with my nephew and his wife. We had a blast!

We worked together making Valentine's strawberries & henny orders. One thing about her is that she is a natural born hustler. That girl always has a plan for us to get a bag, and I was all about it. Just that quick things started getting rocky, month after month she kept losing another loved one. With each loss, I lost another piece of her.

She started getting angrier and angrier and it was harder and harder to have conversations with her. But we continued to work through it, because she never had a problem saying I am sorry. I would tell her how yelling had affected me in the past and how it affected me when she did it, but I realized that she was hurt.

April came around the corner quickly, and after eleven months in prison my husband was released. We were not together, and he was clear about my relationship with my girlfriend. I helped him while he did his bid. I am heavy on the do unto others, what you want done to you. I did not care about the past, all I wanted was to have peace and be a good friend. Now that he was released my two youngest and I were there for him.

Chapter 21

The day came when he was released, my youngest daughter and I went to the local bus station to see if we found him. I hadn't talked to him in over a month, that's when he told me the time he was supposed to arrive at the bus station. His pride wouldn't let him ask for help, and life had taught me up to this point to be there for those who need you regardless of your relationship. Regardless of who you're with. You never know when you're going to need someone. I still stand by these words today more than ever.

When we got there, he was standing alone, under the tree. I could see he had no direction. He looked so lost; it broke my heart immediately. When we pulled up, he was shocked, his face was pale. He later told me he felt like God had sent him an angel. My daughter jumped out and hugged her daddy. I could see how happy she was, it was exactly what she needed with everything going on in our lives. She has always been her daddy's little girl since he was the only father she knows. I could see how awkward he looked, I understood, it was awkward for me too. I jumped out and quickly gave him a hug and broke the ice with a big "Welcome home my dude!!!"

It was a lot for me to take in, it had been two years since the last time we saw each other. I was grateful that I was with someone for the first time that truly trusted me, and although I am pretty sure it bothered her that I was around my ex, she never questioned me, and I respected her even more for it. I just wanted to be there for him, because I knew he had no one else but my daughters and me. Only the two youngest, my oldest daughter no longer wanted to have a relationship with him. She warned me that he would do something against me again. It didn't matter how much I believed that he changed, he had not. But I did not listen.

We arrived at my house, and he just sat on the porch. I knew he didn't want to go inside, and I understood. I warmed up some left over from the night before and brought him out a plate of food. I let him stay with us, with the understanding that it wouldn't be long. Also, that we would respect each other for the time he was staying. He appreciated the favor.

It wasn't long before he would repay that favor. I was dressed and ready for work, rushing out the door for my shift. I also wanted to clean up in the kitchen before I left. I have a bad habit of doing too much all the way to the last minute. If I could get those dishes before I left I would do them, or take out the trash, and I was running around like a chicken with my head cut off once again.

We will call my husband my friend from this point on, since we were not living as a couple any longer. We were barely interacting, and it was awkward between us, so I wanted to hurry out the door. He knew I was running behind, so he got up and said, "don't worry about that I got it, I am going to clean all that for you, just go to work!"

I thanked him and as I was about to run out, I slipped, and just that quick I was laid out on the floor screaming! He ran to me immediately, since he knew I had torn my ACL some years before in one of our fights. I was in excruciating pain, and he quickly picked me up, put me in my truck and rushed me to the ER.

I cried the whole way there, I had nerve damage and could not even bend my leg, walk, anything. I went from running ten hours a night drawing blood, to being told that I would be needing full time care. I sat there in complete disbelief! What was I going to do now? My kids were all out of the house, except for one and she was never home.

I had no family close to me, my girlfriend was in Jersey, the only person left was him. I called him to come back to pick me up, when he arrived, I was so upset. He asked me why I was crying, and I told him that I would not be able to take care of myself and I had no one. He immediately told me he had my back and that he was going to take care of me. He told me that he wanted to. That he wanted to show his appreciation for me having his back. I just sobbed and thanked him. I believed he changed, and that he was sincere, so I accepted his offer to help me. The situation was deeper than the nerve damage, let me explain what taking care of me entailed.

My house was built in 1960 and they did not disclose that I had copper pipes when I purchased the property. A year in the house all my pipes busted, I had water damage, mold, and an eighty-dollar water bill that went up in four months to over two-thousand dollars. I quickly contacted an attorney, who came out and took my case. Unfortunately, the only way he would take my case was, if I did not fix the pipes. So, I would have to live without water in my house.

The attorney also told me that it could be up to a year or even longer. The world was also completely frozen due to covid-19 and that would make everything take longer. I agreed. Growing up in Trenton, I knew I could survive anything. That was nothing, "I got this!" I told myself at the time, "I will go fill my gallons of water, I will figure all this out, it's a small thing to a giant like me!"

Well, that was when I was able to care for myself, but now I could not even go to the bathroom on my own. That is why they say be careful how you do people, you never know when you will need them. That is a fact! When I was there for people, I did it because that was in my heart, no expectations, BUT GOD!!!!!

Now I could not shower or anything alone, plus I had no water in my house, I could not go back to work, and I was alone. That was the beginning of a journey that would change me forever! Immediately, things went from hi and bye, super awkward, to carrying me to the toilet. All over my walls were my pictures with my girlfriend. We were always on the phone, video chat but he put his feelings aside to be my friend and to take care of me when NOONE else did! It is a truth that many will not want to hear but it is the TRUTH! It was only him who went to fill my twenty gallons of water after a long day of work!

I have this down to a science to flush the toilet. I use three gallons, that was three gallons he carried to flush for me daily. For me to bathe he would boil me two gallons and carry the pot to me then get another gallon to add for the perfect temperature. Again, I have it down to a science. After he prepared everything, he then had to come carry me, help me get undressed, pick me up, put me over the tub as I screamed and cried because I could not bend my leg, then to help me take a bath.

After barely not seeing me in two years, I was in so much pain I could not even think about awkwardness. But I repeated over and over how grateful I was. I kept thanking him, and he kept telling me "Don't worry about it, you did more for me!" As he carried me back to my bed and helped me get dressed. In the beginning, I did not tell my girlfriend that it was him taking care of me, and it was not because I was lying about him, it was because I did not want her to have the feelings that I knew came with that type of information.

I was around long enough to know how quick things change when insecurities creep in, and I was protecting our relationship. For the first time someone trusted me, and I did not want to lose that. But quickly I told her. Just how I imagined immediately everything changed. No longer did she stay on the phone with me all day and all night, now she was shut down and barely wanted to talk. I found myself alone, depressed, crying, with only God!

That is exactly where he wanted me! In a place where he can get my attention, I was so far from him, but then again, I was so close. I had to wait until he got out of work so that I could shower. I was so grateful that someone was there after being home all day alone. I saw what my real reality could be. Seemed like every time my desperation started to hit, he would come in and take care of me, I was beyond grateful.

My relationship with my girlfriend was not getting any better, especially with covid-19 no one was allowed to travel. That was her reason for not coming to take care of me and I went with it, even though inside I was really hurt. I felt that if it were the other way around, I would have been there. I just kept pushing, the loneliness and the feeling of abandonment from the people I loved the most was breaking me in a way that I needed to be broken.

I really appreciated the friend I found in the person that I was married to for twenty years. I never imagined we could be at this place. After so much hurt and trauma. I never thought he would be all I had, when he was the person I even journal about a year ago. I was saying how grateful I was, he could never hurt us again, and here he was saving me. We got to know each other like total strangers, he was not the same person I knew, prison changed him. That is what I believed based on his actions.

While he was in prison, he told me he found Jesus, and he found forgiveness. He told me he learned how to love himself so he had let go of all those insecurities that would cause him to disrespect me like he did in the past.

When things couldn't get any worse it hit my house, Covid-19. I tested positive on June 28, 2020, he tested negative. I ended up in the ER and had an extremely tough time with covid. I remember I had to stop halfway to take a breath, the shortness of breath was bad, the red eyes, no taste, no smell, fever, and cough that came along. I was so scared, but more than scared I was so lonely and depressed it seemed like I was never going to reunite with my girlfriend. I, like many people, could not see my children or grandchildren. It seemed like when I was feeling at my lowest point, God always found a way to turn that thing around!

I was sitting around when my friend hit me up about a dog she found in Tampa, and since I have always been the neighborhood animal rescue, at the perfect moment I became the proud momma of the most anxious, craziest dixie pin! My baby girl, Zaza, came to my life to drive me insane at the perfect moment. I love her to pieces, it is the way she hugs me when I need it the most for me!

The world is going insane! It looks like we went back in time, back to Martin Luther King Jr and Malcom X days! Not even my disability was going to stop me from going out there to march! BLACK LIVES MATTER and our voices needed to be heard, so my youngest and her dad took turns pushing my rented wheelchair as we marched through Vero!

It was one of the most empowering moments of my life! I'm so grateful to have shared that special moment in history with my daughter! She will always be able to say she marched for her people, and her mother was a humanitarian that stood up and spoke out!! We were able to take a historical picture that I know she will treasure forever, and I know that I will always carry it close to my heart.

It was August 2020, and I was finally able to walk, then I got the call that my childhood best friend passed away! I had not talked to her in years. When we recently spoke, I promised to visit, and I did not. I missed the opportunity that would not come back in this lifetime. I was broken. I got in my car and drove with my Zaza all the way back home to Jersey!

I was able to see my girlfriend after so long also. With everything that was going on I could not wait to see her, and I had grand expectations for this visit. Things had been off for some time, and I just wanted us to get right. I finally arrived at her house after driving sixteen hours dealing with the loss of my friend, in the middle of a hurricane. I did not realize there was a hurricane hitting at the same time I would be driving and when I realized it, I was in too deep. Thankfully, I made it. I was expecting this big hug and kiss, after hearing all I have been through, and not seeing me in so long but it was all the contrary no hug, no kiss, nothing.

I was not there for five minutes and I wanted to go. I sat on the porch alone smoking a cigarette, crying, and questioning myself. Why did I come all the way here, in so much pain because my leg had not fully recovered, just to feel more alone than I did at home? I could have stayed in Trenton; she lived an extra hour away. I could have spent the time with my childhood best friend, we had lost a sister. Now we were two and instead of being by her side, I came here to be hurt. I went to bed and the next morning we got into an argument, and I was angry to say the least! I was not going to deal with this after I went through all that to get there, so I grabbed my things and left.

I drove down the street to get dressed and brush my teeth out of my car, I left her house in pajamas to avoid any real arguments. I was so upset, but I was not going to keep begging her to show me love during my storm. She quickly called and apologized, and I decided to give it another try. This girl had no clue how hard it was for me to move around and walk but she acted like I was perfectly fine. I couldn't even get in and out of the shower just a week before. The next few days my girlfriend kept showing me her selfish ways, and the more she did, the more I wanted to go home.

It was sad because we had some good moments, but those hard moments were harder for me than any others. I didn't even make it to my friend's funeral and that really hurt me more than I could ever put into words. It was time for me to come home and I was sad but ready to get back. A few days after arriving, I had to drive to Texas to pick up my mother. After so long with no communication, I was more than happy to drive to pick her up. My daughter was pregnant with her third baby, my grandson! My mother wanted to come and help with the baby. So, my nephew and I took the long trip through hurricane Laura.

That was one strong hurricane, she left her mark everywhere she touched. The damage was horrific, I could not believe what I was seeing, this was something you see on T.V. reminded me of Katrina. For my mom I would do it over and over again. I was simply happy to be around her. I praised my God! As I think of the beautiful moments on that drive, I praise him still. Forever my lady in red.

September rolled around and it was my birthday month, so my girlfriend made plans to come down. I was excited, we would go down to Miami with her friends. There we would celebrate her best friend's birthday also. My aunt passed away and that was a big loss for me. My aunt was a big part of my life, and it came so unexpected. I was still trying to have an enjoyable time, in between all the arguments and all the awkward moments we were having. Her friends were amazing, we were having a wonderful time! We were eating pizza and dancing in the street! We were having a blast. But it would not be long before that would end. We were on the beach when I got word that my daughter was in a five-car accident, four cars hit her car from behind. The insane part was, I didn't even react when I got the call!

I already knew that would happen. See, on my way down to Miami the spirit had warned me all about it and even told me her friend would call, and she did. I was told not to worry, that all would be well, and it was. God was too real and too good! After the weekend in Miami, she and I went back to my house for another week and a half. I was hoping that things would get better with us, but it just seemed worse.

 No matter how much I tried I could not knock down the walls she had built since she lost her best friend and all those after. Her pain would not allow her to allow me to come in, and with all the pain I was carrying, it was a ticking time bomb. She went back home, and we did not even sleep in the same room the night before she left. Things were so broken, we both cried the whole way to the airport, and even worse when we said goodbye. Things were worse than we both were ready to admit.

I finally went back to work after being out for four months and I was ready! I was finally feeling back to life, things were not good between us, but we were still holding on. After waiting for so long without income, God blessed me with a financial blessing. Since God blessed me, it would be my opportunity to bless my friend for having my back.

I used some of my blessing to get him his own home. The blessing was not only for him, but it was also a blessing for me too. I had somewhere I could shower and get water from. Our friendship was stronger than ever, that is what I believed. I was happy to be able to bless the person who carried me when I could not walk at all. My grandson was born, and I was on top of the world! Everything was exactly how it should be.

When out of nowhere Jersey called me, he wanted to link up. It had been a minute. Jersey and I went to the beach and we had an amazing conversation, one of forgiveness, gratefulness, and most important healing. I was able to truly forgive myself and forgive him and vice versa.

We left there with a new respect for each other, we had peace and most importantly we both knew that in this life we were blessed to have shared something exceedingly rare. Something that would last a lifetime, and no one could ever take that! We said goodbye and like we always did we saluted! That would be the last time we would see each other.

Two weeks later I got a call at work. It was my big bro asking me if I heard what happened to Jersey, and I asked what he was talking about? Then he told me.... Jersey had passed away. All I remember was screaming!!!! The world stopped. This had to be a nightmare. I had experienced so much loss but this one here hit me differently, this loss would change me in ways that I was not prepared for and continues to change me today.

I was sent home because of how visibly distraught I was. My coworker had to drop me off, I was not even able to drive. I called his brothers in Jersey so that they could tell me it was a lie, they did not. I was devastated! That afternoon I was sitting on the porch with my friend, after a long argument, we were able to come to a mutual respect about the situation, or so I thought.

He was still hurt from the past and I could not understand. That was his feelings and whether he felt some type of way or not I loved Jersey and always will, and nothing or anyone will ever change that. Being in love and loving someone are two separate things and although things didn't work out, I will always love Jersey! Bottom line, that is not something I needed to explain or will ever explain. Jersey will forever be a part of me.

 ASAP that was cleared up.

 I looked up and out of a cloud, white birds began to fly, fly, fly, fly, and fly. There were a number of birds that I had never seen. I still have never seen it again. They continued to fly without letting up and after what seemed forever the last small group landed right across the street and just like that ONE black bird flew in all alone and landed! It was a sign that I could not ignore…. Jersey came by to say goodbye! Just as he had stopped by a few days prior to leaving to warn me, but I did not pay attention.

I was cleaning up a few days before he passed when I bumped into my old bible, I picked it up to move it when a piece of paper fell out. It was a letter I had written to him, it was telling him how proud I was, to continue his path to salvation, and to never give up. Never give up, my favorite words. I stared at it, and I put it back. That day I was having bad chest pains.

The next day I was having the same chest pains when I came into the same bible and again the paper fell out. I read it again and just like that I said I must let go of the past, so I ripped it up in pieces and threw it out. The next morning, I got the phone call, he passed away. The guilt of breaking that paper took a major toll on me, then the birds came to release me and give me the peace that I needed.

After that I was not the same, life suddenly got profoundly serious for me. Even more, life was more painful. Before this, I was living my best life, but after I realized I was living my best lie! Nothing or no one was what it appeared to be.

Chapter 22

The next few months I spent a lot of time with my grandkids. I was trying to keep my mind busy. I didn't want to think of all the losses, I didn't want to hurt, but no matter what I was hurting so bad. I was working, spending time with my friends, and I was yearning for peace. I was in need of something, something only God could give me but still I wasn't ready. I thought the foundation I was standing on was firm, but in reality, it was sand. But GOD!!!!!!

He told me if I would just learn to listen, he would turn my foundation from the sand I was sinking into, to a rock foundation, and NOTHING would be able to move me. My girlfriend and I were working on our relationship, so many plans for our future. We had businesses we were starting together. I was sitting remembering the good times, like our first Valentine's when we worked tirelessly to deliver orders of chocolate covered strawberries. After, we went to New York City where we met with my nephew and had an amazing time.

As I look back, I must be honest with myself. I saw the red flags. She was holding something in, the coldness she displayed was affecting me and my outlook on things. It was making me question our future. Instead of being honest with myself and putting myself in her position, I quickly found fault in her, and continued to push her away.

I always said she was selfish, but the reality was I was just as selfish as she was. I never sat and thought how she must have felt knowing that it was my ex-husband taking care of me when she would give anything to be with me. Her situation didn't allow for her to leave New Jersey, even though she wanted to and reminded me daily. I was helping my Ex financially so that he could be stable and be in a situation where he didn't need my help anymore. I never asked myself how I would feel if the shoe was on the other foot. If it was her helping her Ex, would I be as calm, patient, and trustworthy as she was. I truly doubt that I would.

At the time I wasn't thinking about any of those things. I was too busy helping my Ex, and blinded by the act of kindness that he was displaying while he was in need. I couldn't see her pain; all I saw was her being unsympathetic. Her coldness and her indifference were making me stronger; it was building me up, teaching me to stop being so needy and dependent on someone else's love… I needed to love myself because it was clear I didn't. One day I would thank her, and not blame her. That would come with time, and growth.

My home life was very stressful, it had been for years, my daughters and I had a very rocky relationship. The decisions that I have made in my past have affected them in a very negative way. While I was alone, our relationship was good but when I was around my Ex, or anyone it was a reminder of everything we had suffered. My daughters just wanted me to love myself enough to give myself the opportunity to heal and to be the women that they saw inside me, unfortunately I couldn't see it.

I gave so many years, and so much of my time trying to save others, and trying to save relationships while all along I was tarnishing my relationship with my daughters. I was seeing the hurt that they had been holding for so long come out, and it truly hurt. I fought and argued with them trying to get the respect that I knew I deserved, because no matter what I did, I was always there. I was always a phone call away. Many times, I rescued my daughters, and all the time they rescued me but the pain couldn't see any of that.

Hurt people hurt people, my children were hurt, now I was feeling the raft of that hurt, they were taking out all their frustrations on me and all the same fighting I did with these men for years, I was doing with my true love, my only love, my girls. It was always us… so many years and it had always been us. They are my biggest blessing and for so long I couldn't see it. Sometimes we think just because we are there, we are there. But that's just a lie we tell ourselves.

How many times do we sit around on our phones, or tell them to hold on when they want to talk because we are giving someone else attention? I was guilty. Looking back at my life my biggest regret was not staying alone with them. If I was strong enough to make it, I would have avoided so many heartaches for all four of us, but we can't look back!

ALL THINGS GOD USES FOR OUR GOOD NOT SOME!

As I look back, I realize that everything we went through made three strong, independent, God-fearing women who I am blessed to call my girls. My life would continue to affect them, because what I didn't realize is that if I hurt, they hurt. The next few months would do nothing but hurt. Even if you don't realize it at the moment, hurt is good. Hurt will make you see things you could never see if you didn't go through the test. The test is the testimony. Without the test there is no testimony.

Almost five months had passed since I had seen my girlfriend, so I planned a Valentine's Day visit. We always try to spend the holidays together and I was missing her something crazy, although we were fighting all the time; we had built a friendship! A bond!

We spent most of our day texting, calling, and video chatting. I wanted to make things right, I wanted us to get back the way we were before my ex came back in the picture. I was constantly asking her to show me some affection, and I know she tried because I would be a liar if I said she didn't, but the emptiness that she was feeling was overflowing all over our relationship.

February finally came around and I flew to Jersey to spend Valentine's Day with her and I was determined to relight the fire. I would give it my all and see what happens. I arrived at her house after being lost in an uber for two hours, and already the tension was high. I just wanted to be with her. I missed her so much.

I arrived to a quick kiss and she quickly went and grabbed my bags from the trunk. I knew it was not the welcome I expected after five months, but I ignored it. We went down to her place, where her friend was waiting to meet me. It was so nice to have someone excited to see me! Her friend hugged me tighter and showed me more excitement than my girlfriend and I was feeling the sting.

Her friend quickly offered me a shot, and I just tried to have a good time. I started giving my girl all the things I bought for her and she gave me my gifts as well. Her friend and I just talked and talked for about thirty minutes. All positive vibes. Then everything changed, my girl wanted to go get her car, and she had a ride coming to take us to pick it up. I was irritated at the fact that after traveling so far to come see her, in the snow, it was cold, and I had just been lost for two hours. Now we had to go on a mission as we call them.

 I didn't understand why I wasn't walking into a place with rose petals all over the floor, candles, and a romantic evening just the two of us? I haven't seen you in five months and things are rocky already. Why not put effort into our relationship? I asked myself. The year before she had put so much effort into making Valentine's Day so special, actually she did for every occasion. I was taken back by how much she had changed. She was hurt but I did not notice, in my mind it was all about me.

I stayed quiet, and I went with her. We picked up the car, and I drove. We went to her friend's house to drop something off, when the jeep stopped working. I knew that wasn't going to go well, she could not handle pressure at all. I was right. Immediately she started screaming all crazy. We switched seats, and she started trying to get the gears to change but they were stuck, and when she couldn't get it to move, she started punching the steering wheel. I was not going to deal with that negativity, because I already had my mind made up that if this weekend was bad, it was over. I was tired of giving my years, time, and youth to others and coming out empty. The crazy thing was, our relationship was not like this before. We were always happy and always working together. Things were completely different.

The minute she started punching I put my headphones in and started watching my Chinese soaps, yes, I am addicted. She pulled my headphones out my ear and asked me if I was just going to watch my soaps, and I responded with a quick "Yes!", as I proceeded to put my headphones back on. After two hours we finally got the car running and we went back to her house. She told me to get dressed so we could go out to dinner and I told her I wasn't going anywhere. I was tired first of all. Second, it was snowing, it was cold, and she had just screamed and yelled like a maniac for an hour after not seeing me for five months.

I was starving and I just wanted to shower and eat. She told me that she was going to get us food and make a few quick stops and that she would be back. I showered, I got myself together, and I waited. She called me twice to tell me that she was coming, that she was waiting for my food, after four hours she returned but I was already asleep.

 She woke me up when something accidently hit my head, while she was emptying her pockets. I got up and that's when I noticed she could barely stand, she was drunk. I had never in the almost two years we dated, seen her that drunk. I looked at the time and it was after midnight, she left to go get our food at eight-thirty, was she serious? I thought to myself.

I had enough! I got up and went to the other room to pack my stuff, just before I walked out, I warned her, "I am so pissed right now, just please don't follow me!" She of course followed me anyway, and I just started packing my stuff. I was sitting on the floor attempting to hurry up and shove all my things that I had taken out only a few hours prior to this incident, back in my suitcase. As I was finishing up, she kicked my suitcase, and told me I wasn't going anywhere. I just asked her again to please leave me alone, I could feel myself sweating which is never a good sign, that's that incredible hulk right there! I told you in the beginning of the book. It went well with my personality. I was still trying to maintain my composure, but she wasn't letting up or letting me go.

I called her mom because I didn't know what else to do at this point. I had never been in this situation with her and I could feel that it wasn't going to end well. Her mom was really upset that she was acting this way, her mom and everyone knew how much we loved each other. This was not normal for us. As soon as I got off the phone, she yelled "YOU CALLED MY MOM?" That quick, our relationship went from fixable to what I believed would be unrepairable.

She swung and hit me on my arm. It wasn't the hit that hurt me, it was the person swinging. How could someone that I cared about so much, that I loved so hard do this? She was my best friend, the person I trusted and held on a higher standard than anyone else because she had never done anything like this before. This was a person who I trusted and for the first time I felt free, and this felt right. How could it turn out so wrong. From the alcoholic uncle who molested me and took my childhood. It seemed that alcohol was always involved in my worst moments.

I grabbed her by the hair and threw her into some stuff that was in a corner, I stood over her and warned her not to do that again, that there was a side of me she had never seen, and I didn't want her to see that person! She didn't listen, she got up and swung on me again! This time I put hands on her, but it hurt me more than it could ever hurt her, that was the side of me I never wanted her to know. Even more painful, from my own past I already knew that once you cross these levels of disrespect there is no coming back.

I let her up and asked her not to come chase me; I had my nephew on the phone and he was going crazy! My children may give me all kinds of hell but when it comes to me, they do not play. He was yelling and screaming, I was pulling my suitcase up the stairs trying to get out. Finally, I was outside walking out in the cold, trying not to fall in the snow, while dragging my suitcase, carrying my phone and my purse. While calling her mom to come and pick me up.

Out of nowhere, I felt a fist in my eye and my forehead and I lost it! I forgot about everything that had to do with love, friendship, anything. It was "F" all that!!! I just went in, all face shots, then I realized what I was doing and quickly just grabbed her and started to cry on top of her, asking why? why? why? Why would she hurt me this way? Why would she make me put my hands on her? Why would you make me hurt you? I was broken, and I was done. I stood up and tried to grab my suitcase, but she wouldn't let me, so I left it and walked out front to wait for her mom. She followed me and swung on me again not once but twice, this time I was so over it, I just ate it and walked away. That was a small thing to a giant like me, I just needed to get out of there and never look back again.

Her mom and stepdad came and picked me up and took me home with them. I sat up all night with her mom crying. I cried, and she cried. Her mom loved me so much and did nothing but show me that love and now she sat here broken hearted with me also. I lost a girlfriend, and she was scared that she had lost a daughter. Over and over, I reminded her that nothing will ever change between us, and I've kept my word till this day she is still my mom too. That morning my girlfriend started blowing up my phone asking me where I was? She didn't remember anything that happened the night before. She came over there wanting to fix things, and I knew she felt bad but the damage was done.

As bad as I wanted to stay and fix things, my life experience showed me that it was time to go. So, I left. I got in an uber and went back home to Trenton where my cousins wiped my tears and got me through until Monday when I got on a plane and came home. Moment of impact, I knew at that moment that I wasn't the same person that went to Jersey. I came back a new me, determined to change my life once and for all. I came home and I wasn't progressing at all. I was supporting everyone around me with their goals and it was such a blessing to be a part of that, but just like everything in life all things must come to an end.

I started realizing that I wasn't growing, progressing, I had gotten everything that I could get from this level and I was either going to stay stuck or I was going to elevate. I started reading my bible daily, and most importantly I began praying again. I started to ask God to remove anyone around me who was not for me or of him so that I can find my purpose. I was lost again, I was feeling closed in, stressed out, constantly battling with the person that I thought was my friend.

My ex. Every day I was sitting outside from the time I woke up smoking cigarettes, thinking about my mother not speaking to me, my sisters not speaking to me, my daughters and me not speaking, and some disrespectful, and all not right. I had helped my ex get on his feet. Now he made it clear he didn't want me around anymore. I was in his way since I was staying over there so I can shower, and have water and a kitchen. My house has nothing, no water, no sinks, no furniture, just my bed and personal items. It was a blessing to have somewhere to cook and shower.

Now I was feeling what I made others feel when they lived with me and I made them feel uncomfortable because they didn't clean up or something petty now that I look back. Now I was the one in someone's house feeling some type of way. It was a hurt that I had to feel, I was at my rock bottom once again. No job, no money, and the world is against me. But God!!!

When I felt like giving up, he showed up to save me. I got a call that my sister's mom passed away and I immediately jumped on a flight to Jersey so that I could supposedly be there for my sister in her time of need. Little did I know it would be the other way around. My sister was going to be there for me. My sister and I bonded on a level that I could never imagine. We slept together, something we hadn't done since we were children. We laughed all night, I don't think we slept the whole time but a few hours. We went out for our first girl's day, we had smoothies, got our nails done, and even had a playa bowl, the best acai bowl I've ever had.

We went to Dave & Buster's where we acted like kids playing games and giggling like two little girls who were robbed from each other. I was still dealing with all the baggage I brought with me and my sister started to notice that I wasn't eating. I had stopped eating a long time before I came to Jersey and I had lost so much weight that she was concerned. My sister walked in her room where she found me in tears and she just hugged me and hugged me while I let all that pain and anguish that I was holding in for so long out. My sister grabbed me by the arm and walked me to a wall full of scriptures that my niece had posted when she still lived at home. One by one she made me read them out loud and I did!

After, my sister prayed over me and immediately I felt the love of Jesus over me. Immediately, I started receiving God's peace along with his holy spirit. He said he would leave us a helper, and as soon as my sister interceded for me there was a breakthrough. I had allowed myself to run from God when I needed him the most. It was time to get back to my first true love. It was time to reach out to my father!

Chapter 23

My nephew came to pick me up so we could go to dinner, since I would be heading back to Florida soon. We hung out like we always do, that's my boy. He's my nephew, my son, but he's also my best friend and my biggest fan and vice versa. We went back to his house to pick up his wife and I told him that I was going to stay outside. I lit a cigarette and I looked up; the sky was full of stars.

I was taken back; the sky was amazing. I was in awe, I even forgot about the cigarette, it was just burning in my hand. I started talking to God and praying to him, asking him to help me find my purpose. Asking God to lead me, to help me get out of this place that I found myself once again. Just like that, I heard it loud and clear, "You are purposed to go out into the world and show people who I truly am!" "You are purposed to go and clean the earth and get it ready for my return" he gave me a clear vision of where I was to start! The cleanup needed to start with me.

I came home and I started to pray that he would take these cigarettes off me. I prayed that he would lead my every step and just like that within a few weeks he did. April 11, 2021, I began to write this book led by the holy spirit. I cried so many times wanting to quit. Knowing that I was putting out all my dirty laundry and that of those that I love, BUT GOD!!!!

I was just about to quit, but instead I begged God to give me a sign of what to do. I was walking into the gas station and just like that I heard him again clear as day! "This book has nothing to do with you, this book has everything to do with me!" "This book is going to teach people all over the world who I really am and how much I truly love every one of you! This book is for the victims, for the hurt people who need to know that I am real and that I will use every hurt, every tear, every pain, and every disappointment, for their good! FINISH THE BOOK! Don't worry what people may say I have you, I always have."

At the moment, I realized that this book was and is needed! This book is the only way that people will finally understand that God is not a God who is looking at our sins. God gave his only begotten son so that we could be free from sin, and that all who believe in him would have life! The problem is that people stopped believing in Jesus, they stopped believing because of hurt, of pain, the loss of a loved one, even their own sin. People have walked so far off from him and are afraid to come to him for the same sins he died for.

Jesus has shown me over and over that he is for me!! Jesus has shown me that all he wants me to do is TRUST HIM!!!! BELIEVE IN HIM!! HAVE FAITH!!!!

For each of us to know that no matter how small or how big our situation is, that he is there and that he is actively working for our good. Trust the process. He wants us to forgive one another but most importantly to LOVE one another freely just as he has forgiven and loved us!

So many people are holding on to hurt for years. Sadly, they can't be around people who hurt them, can't even move forward in their lives because of pain that they can't let go of! The sad truth is, the forgiveness they are holding is not for the accusers, it's for themselves! Writing this book, I realized the only person I needed to forgive was me!

I was holding on to so much guilt, I couldn't even look at myself, let alone love myself!! I had to forgive myself for all the men I laid up with, but threw this book God gave me the real truth! I was seven years old the first time a man treated me like a woman, he didn't ask my permission, I didn't even know what was going on, and he continued to do so until the young age of nine.

How was I supposed to know that it was okay to say no? How was I supposed to know that when a man wants to lay with you, you just don't lay there and comply? How was I supposed to know better? I couldn't. Since I was seven, I believed that you pleased a man when he asked and that was our purpose. I now own my truth, I now know that this is my body, through this book I realized that no one and I mean no one has the right to take anything away from you! Especially not YOU from yourself!

We are our own worst critics! People took everything away from me, and I in turn took everything away from others, especially my daughters. Even more, I took everything away from myself! But God!!!

 Hurt people hurt people! But Jesus can repair every hurt! There is no hurt too big or too small for Jesus to repair. These last few weeks my book seemed to be going in slow motion, but that's how I knew that God was in full control and that it was him taking the lead!

Once again, I was hurt, this hurt was "The Hurt!" The much-needed hurt! Hurt comes with a purpose, every hurt comes with a lesson and a blessing. Look for it. This was the hurt that would change me! I ended up all alone in my house again. I was going to get my water daily. In this empty house I found myself at a crossroad. I was in desperate need of love. I was just like this house, broken and falling apart.

Then I heard God and he promised me that "When he gets through with me, when he gets through nailing on me, when he gets through hooking up my two-by-fours together, and putting my windows up! When he gets through hanging my siding, and placing bricks on my frame! Then I am going to be a glorious building, a sight for the world to see!" But he made it very clear this house is not for me to be glorified, but that GOD will be EXALTED and GLORIFIED!

It is God, through his Word, speaking into existence his will, not my will. I am so glad beyond words that it is God and not man that is in full control of my future and my purpose! I wouldn't want any man to have the power to determine my future! If it was a man, I myself would probably be nailed to a stake. I went through different places of worship, and in those hospitals for the sick, I became sicker! I found no healing where there was still hurt, and I realized that if I didn't set out to get to know God for myself, it would cost me my life.

I serve the God of Moses, of Isaac, of Abraham, of David, of Daniel, and no one can take him from me. I praise and worship daily when I am in my car, in the shower, in the bed, on the phone, it doesn't matter. I praise him because he is good, because he wakes me up daily, because he is here in the midst of my storm when no one else is!

I had folks walk through my house, see my conditions and walk right out, judging me because I had a praise and the name of Jesus in my mouth, but he stood behind me! Jesus is the only reason that I find the most peace in a situation that would break most people.

In this empty house I wrote the story of my life, but the God that I serve gave you the ending first, now he is getting ready to write my beginning, and as I encourage you all to find Jesus, I am beyond humbled to say "EYES HAVE NOT SEEN, EARS HAVE NOT HEARD, ALL GOD HAS PLANNED FOR ME!"

What I will say is, find for yourself that Jesus, the Jesus that got me through the darkest hours of my life. Find the friend that he is! Stop letting people use sin to keep you away from the one who loves you best. Jesus died for those sins; evidence proves they are irrelevant today!!!

Repent daily but never ever stop looking for him, calling on the most powerful name in all the earth! He still is and forever will be in control, there is nothing too big or too small for Jesus! He is and forever will be OUR REIGNING KING! He is on the way back soon, and until he does, I will continue to praise my God and to show love to every single person that stands before me.

Respect, love, and kindness are all free. We are living in historical times. Every day is a new opportunity to be the light in a very dark world. News media as well as social media feeds us anxiety, panic, and fear. In contrast we serve a God that wants to free us from all these things. If we cast our cares and fears upon him, he will in return give us his unending peace. There is hope and our loving father wants us to stand firm on that hope!

I love you all, I pray that you find forgiveness, love, and freedom in the pages of this book and that you never ever forget that Jesus loves you, he is the author and maker of your book, don't let this world take it from you!!!

Don't live to die, but die to live! Self-healing is the best gift we give ourselves! Allowing the love of God to guide us, we are then free to trust, love, and to be truly happy knowing that we are in the best hands.

He is a happy God, and even in a world that looks like everything is coming to an end, it is truly only heading to its beginning. Come back to your first love! Jesus loves you and he is waiting with open arms to bring you into your best season, the one that will produce fruit!

May God bless you and keep you always.

Made in the USA
Middletown, DE
30 November 2025

23533112R00139